MW01172055

Big Boys Do Cry:

A Man's Guide to Navigating Emotions and Showing Up More Vulnerable in Relationships

Ryan Joseph Kopyar

Copyright © 2024 Ryan Joseph Kopyar

All Rights Reserved. No part of this book may be reproduced in any form without permission in writing from the author. Reviewers may quote brief passages in reviews.

Disclaimer. No part of this publication may be reproduced or transmitted in any form or by any means, mechanical or electronic, including photocopying or recording, or by any information storage and retrieval system, or transmitted by email without permission in writing from the publisher.

Table of Contents

Hey, Man

I cry.

Yes, you read that right.

Now, I know what you're thinking… it's an unconventional way to start a book.

Yet, for three decades of my life, this admission would have been inconceivable. So here we are, my biggest "not so secret" out in the open.

I'm leading with vulnerability from the first sentence in the hopes you will join me here. This will serve as our meeting ground to embark on this journey and connect.

You see, I spent so many years of my life not crying.

So much so that I could start this book with, "I didn't cry for 30 years." Once I did, everything changed for me. I unlocked, or maybe the better way to say that is reconnected, to a core aspect of myself that has benefited me as a human in all capacities. As a man, a counselor, a husband, and as a friend.

To achieve that change, I had to allow myself to connect to those thoughts, feelings, and emotions that I had buried inside for so long, ESPECIALLY my pain.

The key word here is ALLOW! I had to give myself permission to access that part, or parts of myself, that had these stored emotions, which then became the catalyst for my tears along with my release and ultimate reconnection to my full range of emotions.

Big Boys Do Cry

My hope and mission here are to open up your mind to what is possible for you. I want you to achieve the same liberation and reconnection to those parts of yourself.

I grew up in a small town in upstate New York called Binghamton in the United States of America with a blue-collar, hardworking family and Western cultural values. Which is to say that crying was not a topic discussed often. It also means, I rarely saw the adult men in my life cry.

This narrative is not unique to my upbringing. The rules of society echo similar sentiments today. Phrases such as "Boys don't cry", "Man up" and even "Stop acting like a p#ssy!" are still prevalent today, and limit the perceived acceptability of it being "ok" for men to have or express a wider range of their emotions.

I saw this stoicism firsthand: my great-grandfather, grandfather, and father—all embodied this unyielding narrative. There was also one exception. My Papa, a toughened army veteran and former New York State Trooper, dared to shed a tear. But more on these men later.

My intention in writing this book is to help men understand how to connect to their feelings. I want you to believe that it is not just "okay" but an amazing ability to have and then learn how to use this ability to show up more vulnerable in relationships, especially with your wives and families.

I am here to advocate that we're not only allowed to have those feelings, but also to honor ourselves for having them. One of the main tasks we have ahead of us is finding reasonable, safe, and healthy ways to express those emotions. It's a hard thing to do when you are feeling angry, sad, unseen, unheard, unsupported, or unrecognized. But, crying is one of the healthiest expressions for all of the above. So, stay with me, and let me show you how and why!

In these pages, I'm going to share the different events in my life where I held back the tears. In some cases, for a long time. I'll also dive into my reliance on substances to numb pain, and how that leads to more blocking and suppressing of emotions.

We will also discuss the "aha" moments in life when we realize how much unnecessary stress, pain, and pressure we carry as men.

You cannot rewrite history, and we cannot go back in time to teach you these skills. But you can give old history a new meaning, and learn new skills today, and through that process, the present is yours to mold. And your future, a better future, awaits. A future that I believe can be filled with deeper levels of peace, love, joy, and happiness. I don't promise to provide you with the solution of how not to experience the antithesis to these emotions, because experiencing the pain, the sadness, the grief, and the anger are all part of what it means to be human. But I will provide a framework on how to navigate these emotions in a healthy and effective way.

My invitation to you as you read this book is to keep an open mind and, even more importantly, an open heart. (Hopefully, this book gets you back into your heart, or in it at a deeper level!)

I hope that parts of my story will resonate with parts of your story.

My story has a bit of everything; pain, struggles, hope, and of course, a whole bunch of my life lessons.

Please realize that you're not alone. So, when you're not feeling seen, heard, or appreciated, it's okay to acknowledge that, to feel it, and then to express that in a healthy way.

Holding on weighs you down.

Holding your pain inside is not what makes you tough.

It's what makes life tough.

That is why the process of releasing the burden of past emotions can be so liberating.

Big Boys Do Cry

Take it from me and my mistakes—I've made a bunch. And I'm human, so I have no doubts that I'm going to continue to make more.

But life is better when we forgive ourselves and others. And that can only be done through acknowledging what it is that we are feeling.

Of course, life won't get magically easier just because we can identify, connect to, and express our wide range of feelings. There are still cycles, ups and downs, joy and pain, emptiness and fulfillment. These are all part of the human experience. But to identify and release those thoughts, feelings, and emotions that no longer serve us, brings balance and understanding which makes life more manageable.

My role in this book is to help you to feel seen and heard. To give you hope that you don't have to keep carrying around these intense emotions and feel like you're hopeless or completely lost on how to get rid of the thoughts, feelings, and emotions that have been weighing you down.

I am driven by the profound belief in your incredible potential. I have seen and also experienced firsthand what happens when people believe in us. When people pour that belief into us, pour hope into us, and make us feel that change is possible, and healing is possible.

I've been fortunate to have such individuals in my life, guiding me with tools and knowledge. But I must say that the crucial part for me was taking those tools and then implementing them, as I proceed forward with my ongoing journey towards healing. I had a few people who believed in me, instilled hope, and equipped me with skills I hadn't learned as a little boy. Ultimately, I believe that by evolving into a better version of yourself, you enhance every facet of your life—be it as a husband, father, uncle, coach, employer, employee, cop, firefighter, farmer, or in any role you fulfill. This book is my attempt to instill hope in you, to reaffirm that change is achievable and that you possess the ability to heal and transform, regardless of your current position. There's boundless potential for life to get better for you, regardless of where you stand today. And know that no matter where you are, healing and learning are continual parts of an ongoing journey. I share this because, even with all the work that I have done to get to this point, I aspire to consistently evolve and grow along these paths. (Heck, I have even grown while writing this book!)

This book poured out of me, and with the guidance of my editor, I managed to finish it in just shy of 2 months. I don't share this to boast, but to convey the immense passion I hold for the content within these pages. My fervor stems from a belief in the possibility of change, healing, and growth for individuals. It's a conviction that everyone can evolve into a better version of themselves. I wholeheartedly feel it's my life's purpose to be open and vulnerable, aiding men in improving how we navigate our emotions and relationships.

To all my brothers out there:

I see you.

I hear you.

I honor you.

I invite you to come on this journey with me and to be open to the possibility of a couple of tears. This is the path of vulnerability and strength. On that path, life gets lighter, joy becomes even more blissful, laughs get deeper, relationships get stronger, and love, not only for others but also our self-love, becomes abundant.

My Counseling Journey

The year is 2019, and I'm still very much in the depths of recovery from a serious car accident that has affected me mentally, emotionally, and physically. Multiple tears in my rotator cuff and herniated discs make exercising, my former emotional outlet, quite challenging. I've put on some love handles (damn I don't like these!) nothing drastic, but it's unfamiliar, affecting my self-image and how I feel about myself. I'm currently on disability pay, which is only 60% of my previous income. Financially strained, paying off debts would almost wipe out my bank account. To top it all off, I am in an unhealthy relationship where love seems absent, and anger seems pervasive. That's where I'm at, and it feels like rock bottom, or close to it.

Just one year before that in 2018, I faced a whole different set of life struggles that while brutal, showed me I can make it through tough times. I discuss this part of my journey more in my first book, *Unlock the Power of Your Mind.*

Now back to the present moment. It's a beautiful spring morning in May 2019, and I'm on my couch, embracing my prayer and meditation, which I learned as new emotional outlets since my gym time was limited. Suddenly, the feeling of intuitive knowing hits me—"I should go back to school for psychology." This thought was a surprise, not a conscious idea, yet it felt oddly significant. It came on so strong and so powerful that I knew I had to follow it.

The same day, I got a DM on Instagram from a friend. He had just started working as a marketing consultant for a counseling practice nearby and wanted to gain more followers. I noticed on the social media page that the practice specialized in hypnotherapy. Just the day before, (you'll come to realize that I don't believe in coincidences) another friend who is a therapist, had been explaining to me that childhood trauma, including the loss of my mother and unborn sister, could have exacerbated my PTSD after the car accident, and that hypnotherapy was something that could help me on my healing journey.

The next day, I met the counselor from that counseling office, Billy. Of course, it was no coincidence that Billy worked out at the 24-Hour Fitness where I made my part-time return to work. I truly feel as though the Universe was perfectly lining up my healing journey. Although I didn't even realize at that time just how magical and transformative this healing journey would be. After a 10-minute talk with Billy at the gym, we scheduled our first counseling sessions together.

There was one particular moment in our first session together which I will never forget. After going into the hypnotic state, Billy instructed me to raise my right arm in the air. Billy guided me, and we worked through releasing the pain and the trauma which I had been holding on to for so long.

Man, it felt like my arm was up for so long, and at the same time, I felt like so much of this pain and trauma that I had stored inside my body was releasing.

As that release happened, Billy instructed me to allow my arm to naturally go down by my side. I don't even know if I can fully put into words the transmutation and release that I felt happening. I should also note that I can understand that what I am describing may sound like a relatively simple or even arbitrary action of holding your arm up and then letting it down, but it was a physical representation of the connection to and release of my pain and trauma.

Big Boys Do Cry

Suffice it to say, my sessions with Billy were transformative. Through Billy's unique combination of talk therapy and hypnotherapy, Billy helped me in the process of changing my life. It was like shedding layers of emotions I'd held onto for too long—grief, abandonment, and a persistent shield of hyper-independence that isolated me. (Shout out to Billy - his being generally cool and into fitness also helped with the bond and safety I felt in exploring those issues. That's why finding a counselor you feel comfortable with is so important!)

Billy's sessions brought profound emotional releases, unblocking years of pent-up feelings.

The walls around my heart began to crumble.

For the first time in so long, I felt seen and heard.

I cried.

I was infused with the hope of healing that Billy instilled in me.

After the first few sessions with Billy, I sat in my car and cried profusely. I was overwhelmed by a rush of thoughts, feelings, and emotions. This is part of the healing process, and I want to normalize that process for you if you decide to engage in counseling.

Billy and I continued our work together for several months. I'm incredibly grateful for all he did for me.

Now here's another plot twist, which I never would have expected, but it ties back to the message about going back to school for psychology. Midway through our sessions, Billy suggested something surprising: he encouraged me to become a counselor. He had noticed my interactions with people at the gym, recognizing my care and compassion. When Billy expressed confidence in my potential as a counselor, I was a bit thrown off. Mind you, I had no idea all that was involved in going back to get your Masters. I had no idea how I was going to be able to pay for it, find the time for it, or even if I was mentally and emotionally ready for it, as I was still in the depths of recovering from my car accident. To this day I can't fully describe exactly what it was, but I just knew that this was something I had to do and without giving it much conscious thought, I followed my gut feeling that seemed to guide me to say, YES!

Billy swiftly facilitated connections and helped to get me enrolled in St. Peter's University for their clinical mental health counseling master's program. It felt like a sudden shift from three decades of healing reluctance to diving into transformative counseling sessions with Billy and pursuing my master's. As someone with a criminal justice degree (which went unused in that field), the idea of obtaining a master's seemed unreal. Yet, Billy's support paved the way for where I am today.

Can you believe that? Going from broken mentally and physically, heartbroken and literally broke, to having someone on your side believing in you and allowing you to achieve real, life-changing goals. I still occasionally message Billy to this day to express my gratitude.

My experiences with Billy reinforced my passion for the power of counseling. Finding the right counselor is a personal journey, and finding a counselor or therapist that you feel comfortable with is critical. I'll share tips at the end of this book on finding the right fit. Opening up about my personal counseling journey vulnerably, I hope it inspires you to consider the life-changing impact counseling can have, regardless of when you start. It took me nearly three decades to begin, but within the first sessions with Billy, I felt a profound internal shift. Healing isn't straightforward. I say that the healing or counseling journey is not linear. There's ups and downs, starts, stops, and pauses. There are times when you feel you've made a tremendous amount of progress, and times when you can feel that you're going backward, it's all part of the healing journey. Even still, I promise you, it's a journey worth taking!

The Men in My Life and What I Learned

Great Grandfather – Joseph

When was the last time you thought about your generational narrative? If the answer is never, that's ok. For now, I will simply say this, the stories and dynamics of our past are relevant to how we think about ourselves and life today.

Great-grandpa Joe's age made our time together limited. I recall moments spent at his house, with him watching wrestling through binoculars due to his failing eyesight. He might have been old, but he wasn't about to quit his favorite pastime. Despite my young age, I observed the interactions between my great-grandfather, my grandfather, and sometimes my father with intense curiosity.

The tension between my great-grandfather and my grandfather was evident. Later in life, stories emerged—of my great-grandfather hoarding food in his room when he moved in with my grandparents. (I can only imagine the level of dysfunctional communication that must have been occurring as it relates to keeping food in his bedroom and not in the kitchen!) Suffice it to say, my grandpa Art, had a rocky relationship with his father. And as far as I ever came to understand it, my grandpa spent more time being raised by his grandparents than he did with his mother and great-grandpa Joe. My grandpa Art even lied about his age so that he could move out of his childhood home and join the United States Navy.

Reflecting on their dynamics, I couldn't help but ponder the difficulties my grandfather faced—struggles that likely carried through generations. It dawned on me that Great-grandpa Joe perhaps lacked the tools to impart love, communication, or vulnerability to my grandfather. Was he ever allowed to cry? I highly doubt it. More questions soon emerged. How far does this storyline extend? Was my great-great-grandfather similar? Well, probably, yes!

Though I won't dwell long on Grandpa Joe, his context becomes pivotal in understanding the impact of other men in my life—my grandpa Art, and my father, Joe. It also serves as my starting point.

As men, this exploration of the men who raised us holds immense significance. Often, we look up to our fathers as role models or ideals for how to behave. Whether it's a forced emulation, natural admiration, or even unconsciously learned behaviors, much of our behavior and interactions stem from these paternal figures. Even if you had an absent father figure, that gap sets a standard of behavior that creates its own set of challenges.

Papa - Doug

If we are fortunate in life, we have one or two people who make us feel deeply loved and cherished. For me, that person was my papa, my mom's father - Papa Doug for me, Douglas Lourmond Gell, for the world.

From a young age, Papa made me feel incredibly special. One of my favorite childhood memories is him picking me up from school in his pickup truck and grabbing takeout from my favorite Italian spot, followed by a visit to the Red and White convenience store.

Despite being an Army veteran and later a New York state trooper and having a tough guy exterior, I always knew my Papa as a warm and loving man. In that regard, he was an anomaly. He had this ability to light up a room with his energy and larger-than-life persona. But he also struggled with alcohol use. He sang, he performed, and on multiple occasions I witnessed him shedding tears during heartfelt speeches, particularly at family weddings. At the same time, he looked like a guy you wouldn't want to cross - tall, broad, deep voice, and later in life, with a big belly!

His ability to connect with me emotionally, I believe, was a lesson he learned later in life. And that is a distinction worth noting.

I'm sure that if you asked my aunt and uncles or my grandmother, they may not have described him as such a tender or emotional man for them when they were growing up.

What changed?

My mother's tragic passing, his daughter's, was that event.

Big Boys Do Cry

With my mother gone too soon, I believe my Papa found a new way to honor and love her. That way was through his love for me. His affection for me felt like an extension of his love for his daughter. It created a beautiful relationship.

And as much as he loved me, I loved him so dearly right back. As his health began to decline, and his big belly shrunk, it got to the point where he was so weak he couldn't get off the couch in the living room. I loved my Papa so much that I slept on the ground right next to him on the couch.

For all his love for me and my love for him, we never discussed the biggest connection that we both had to each other. My mother, McKay. One reason for that could be my young age at the time. Maybe that would have changed if we had more time together. But as it stands, there were things left unsaid.

In the final days of his life, when he was at the hospital, I went to visit him. I'll never forget what he told me. Laying in the hospital during his final days, he told me, "Stay away from the booze." At the time, I didn't fully grasp its meaning, heck, I was only about 12. However, later in life, after I struggled with using drugs and alcohol to numb my pain, I came to understand what he meant. I don't know if my Papa was doing the same with his drinking. But I truly feel that in his last breaths of life, he was encouraging me to face my pain rather than to try to numb it.

The truth is, there is so much healing and inner power that comes from confronting our pain instead of numbing it. Confronting our pain means facing it head-on. In therapy, I call it "feeling your feelings." Confronting our pain, our deepest and heaviest emotions, is probably the bravest action you can do. But as men, we are told that to lean into those feelings, or to go to counseling to address our pain, is 'a sign of weakness.' For so long, it has been the stereotype that 'asking for help' means we are weak. So it's no wonder why so many men shy away from this process.

In my professional life, I see this struggle in many of the men I work with. Waiting years to ask for help, using substances, and engaging in addictive patterns — all attempts to avoid the feelings of internal pain. (Trust me, I know the patterns all too well on a personal level.)

I genuinely believe that if you are following along so far, you are likely nodding along, connecting the dots from stories in your generational history, and maybe finding your unique patterns of avoiding your pain.

Hang with me man, because if you're open to it, we're going to be able to make that shift into "feeling the feelings" together.

Grandpa - Art

Let me tell you about my grandpa, Art. Grandpa passed away when I was around 20 or 21. I had a strong bond with him, and he taught me a lot about hard work and advocating for myself. Despite his tough exterior, I was also lucky to see at least one moment of his vulnerability.

You might remember the story about him lying about his age to join the Navy. Think about that! Lying about your age to go and join the Navy while your country is at war. It speaks volumes about the life he must have endured.

It will come as no surprise that Grandpa wasn't expressive emotionally. I never heard him say "I love you" or show much physical affection. He wasn't a big hug guy, either. (He was the guy who recycled birthday cards and kept lots and lots of coupons! My grandma would get a birthday card, saying "Happy Birthday", then grandpa would take it back to give it to her the following year. I swear that was an ongoing family joke!) My Grandpa worked in construction, and there were periods with no work. That intensified the idea that you have to 'pinch pennies' and overall live in a 'scarcity mindset.'

This scarcity transcended into emotions, vulnerability, and outward expressions of love.

It also included relationships.

The common thread here is scarcity.

Ryan Joseph Kopyar

This theme was present in the relationship I saw between him and my father. Reserved, harsh at times, shut down, yet with lots of unspoken love and affection.

There was, however, one time in my life in which I saw my grandpa show his emotion. One Christmas Eve when I was home from college. My grandmother and father had gotten into a pretty heated disagreement, and my grandmother didn't end up coming over for Christmas Eve. This left just my grandpa, my father, my stepmother, and me.

As usual, we exchanged gifts. My grandfather was not a difficult man to shop for, any pragmatic gift would elicit the same response from him: a smile and a "Thank you". But getting him something meaningful was difficult.

That all changed when my father brought out a present that our family friend had stumbled across in a local garage sale. A metal well drilling sign that belonged to the Kopyar family business. It displayed our family name, drilling services, and a phone number with only six digits (yes, it was that old!).

I was curious to see my grandpa's reaction to the special gift, but I did not expect the reaction my grandfather would have.

No words were exchanged as my father handed him the present. As my grandpa unwrapped the sign, there was an impactful silence in the room. The two men stared at each other, with my grandfather clearly fighting back some emotions. A small sign of vulnerability, less than a tear, had appeared on my grandfather's face.

After a long pause, he went on to explain the significance of the sign. In his own words, my grandpa described how the relic encapsulated our family's drilling legacy. (A legacy which he had no interest in furthering.) Could it be because of the absence of his father? Which very likely happened, because great-grandpa Joe was spending so much time working that he wasn't able to be there for my grandpa. Or maybe the

17

reaction was due to a reminder of a life that he could have chosen? Had he kept the business, it would have meant a better and more financially abundant life. It also would have changed the trajectory of his work-life balance and the upbringing my father (and then I) had. The 'ifs' are endless.

Reflecting now, I regret not probing my grandfather's emotions and how they fit into our family's narrative.

My Father – Joe

When it came to my father, his strength was unique. I've only seen him shed tears two, maybe three times in my entire life. He taught me resilience, independence, and the practicalities of running a household. Those pragmatic lessons, the chores, the early mornings, and late nights—my Dad bore it all. For several years, until he remarried, he didn't have a partner to help with raising me after the tragic loss of my mother and unborn sister.

There were a lot of takeout dinners from a local Italian restaurant and a lot of quiet car rides. I could feel his pain, an agony no words can capture and nobody should have to live through. A 23-year-old, losing a wife carrying their eight-month unborn daughter, navigating single parenthood. I sensed his exhaustion, yet we never delved deep into that profound pain or our shared grief. We had little to no conversations during that time about emotions.

I can't blame him; I admire him immensely for his strength in raising me, especially during those early years of my life. His resilience, his sacrifices, his unwavering commitment to being there for me, I admire all of it. But to this day, I can't help but reflect that underneath all of that, there was a lot of unsaid, unexpressed grief and emotions harbored for years.

If I could go back to those quiet car rides, or those dimly lit, late-night dinners, I would say to my father and the younger version of myself, "It's OK to cry. It's OK to acknowledge the loss, it's OK to ask for help." You see because I never had anybody to tell me this. And for nearly three decades, I bottled it all up until I chose healing. It took one decision. The decision to embrace the pain, to begin to let it out.

On the day my grandfather passed away, we received a call while my stepmom, dad, and I were at home. My uncle was visiting because my grandfather's health was deteriorating. My grandmother urgently asked us to come over, unaware that he had already passed.

When we arrived, I found my grandfather slumped over on the couch, lifeless. It was only the second time I had seen my father cry, and the memory is vivid. My grandfather lay on one end of the couch, my dad on the other, and I sat in my grandfather's favorite recliner, trying to process everything. I hadn't dealt with my grief over my mother and unborn sister's deaths at that point, so I was as numb as you can imagine.

Despite all this, I was struck by my father's heartfelt words to my grandfather. My dad, typically reserved, was now openly weeping, expressing his deep love and regret for not having more time together. He called my grandfather his 'best friend' and pleaded for more moments with him. It was a side of my dad I had never seen before—vulnerable and expressing emotions so openly. It was apparent to me that there was quite a bit left unsaid between my dad and my grandpa.

The moment was impactful. Looking back, I see the importance of vulnerability between them. If only my grandfather and father had been more open with each other, sharing those emotions, maybe my dad wouldn't have felt these unfinished sentiments. It made me think about life and death a bit differently.

The truth is, that death is a part of our life story. We can't escape it. Once that arrives, and it will, all the rest goes into the pile of unfinished business, and words left unsaid. The pain, regret, and responsibility of those words have a tremendous impact if you are the one still alive. I know that and see it in my clinical work, with friends, and even myself. The living are left with the knowledge that they could have… but didn't.

Ryan Joseph Kopyar

While I can't speak for all who have experienced loss and tragedy, this to me was an experience that influenced me deeply. The fact that there will come a time when we can no longer say to the person, "I love you." or "I miss you." or "You matter to me."

It also made me realize how what we see is not always as it seems. I saw how my dad's stoic attitude and tough exterior, as well as the fights between him and my grandpa, were only one part of the coin. Under that, there was a lot of emotion and love.

My father's emotional outpouring, in a moment of intense grief, revealed a side of him I hadn't known.

The last thing to remember here is that our stories, including those of our family and our past, hold memories and emotions that shape our legacies. As men, we can rewrite family patterns and set new standards for communication and emotional expression.

I'm sharing parts of my story with so much vulnerability to bring you to that moment, but also to emphasize that it took me time. A lot of time and a lot of my brokenness was needed, to come to the point of being open to healing. There were so many moments that I could have faced the pain, and I didn't. I numbed it, avoided it, and was afraid to lean into it. So, if you are feeling weak or discouraged for not having started your healing journey, please know that it's OK and it's not 'too late.'

Life isn't about changing events because that's not possible. It's about re-shaping the meaning we assign to them. When I finally embraced my brokenness, it allowed me to give it a new meaning,

I've come to realize that sometimes the **H-O-L-E** provides us with an opportunity to become **W-H-O-L-E** again.

If you decide so, this book can be the first step for you to face and embrace your pain. Maybe you can say to yourself, "I'm going to allow myself to cry". This moment will be the one you will allow your mind,

21

body, and soul to experience the pain, without numbing it, like I did. Trust me, it is an integral part of the healing process.

We've got to feel it to heal it.

Now, when I reflect on those silent car rides and dinners with my dad, I understand our silence was not a testament to strength but rather a reflection of the stigma surrounding emotional vulnerability. The pattern that was created, wove a mask that hid all that we didn't want or know how to embrace.

As I conclude, and we start the journey into deeper threads of the human experience and our ability to express emotions, I urge you to think about this.

When you allow yourself to feel, to express, and to heal, you will not just be rewriting your story, you will be rewriting the narratives of generations to come.

Actionable steps

1. **Reflect on connections:**
   - Recall people in your life who made you feel deeply loved or special.
   - Reflect on the moments and interactions that made these connections meaningful.

2. **Evaluate Emotional Bonds:**
   - Consider the role of vulnerability in strong relationships and its impact on connection.
   - Assess how expressing emotions strengthened those bonds and impacted your connections.

3. **Was There a Message?**
   - Evaluate advice or messages from significant figures and their resonance in your life.

- Reflect on how these messages might have influenced your decisions and behaviors.
- Recall "aha" moments and when they emerged.

4. **Recognize Numbing Behaviors:**
   - Acknowledge any tendencies to resort to numbing behaviors to avoid emotional pain.
   - Reflect on the potential for growth and transformation by facing internal struggles directly.

Generational Trauma

Generational trauma isn't a buzzword; it's a very real aspect of the human experience. Unfortunately, the reality of generational trauma is often something we wish we could leave in the past, but can't, until we become aware of it and break free from it.

As an example, imagine your great-grandma, tough as nails, living through some crazy hard times in Brooklyn. She hustled, kept it all inside, never shedding a tear, just grinding through life. She faced poverty, crime, and possibly emotional or physical abuse.

Now, your grandma picks up that vibe and carries it through Queens. She's got that same stoic attitude, with no room for emotions,

Fast-forward to your mom—growing up in Manhattan, she's all about that "tough it out" mentality. She's living by the code, never letting anyone see her sweat. It was what she learned from her mom, and how she models behavior for you. Why is she so guarded and tough? Her life has been pleasant by all accounts: no major struggles, good private education, a 6-figure job.

And then, here you are, with that energy in you, and the associated learned behavior you're now living out. You're carrying that emotional backpack passed down through generations. This generational energy within you feels natural, perhaps unchosen, maybe even subconscious, yet present nonetheless. You start to see in it traits and behaviors that are not well-suited to your life and journey. For us men, this is often a 'tough guy persona,' which causes us to struggle to be vulnerable or create connections in our interpersonal relationships. Especially with those we love the most.

But here's the catch—nobody ever taught you how to unpack it. It's like being handed a map of the city, but nobody tells you how to read it!

This is one way of viewing generational trauma.

The good news is that this isn't about throwing blame around. It's about saying, "Hold up, this ain't on me, and I want to change it!" You can rewrite the script. It's like reprogramming your iPhone and hitting reset.

Our understanding of generational trauma is quite recent. Its presence, however, is not.

It was first discussed during the traumatic aftermath of World War II. Notably, women who endured the Holocaust and became pregnant passed on a heightened risk of stress-related and mental health issues to their children.

Not only that, but having two Holocaust survivor parents, instead of just one, was shown to increase the likelihood of adverse effects even more.

This line of research examines what we now refer to as "epigenetic inheritance", the idea that our environment, especially when traumatic, can live in the body and be passed on to our children, and even grandchildren through our DNA.

So what do I do about it?

Here's the first step, there is no reason to beat yourself up over a programming system you didn't code.

But that begs the question, how do you crack this code? My opinion is you start rewriting the narrative within your head first, with your friends and loved ones second and if possible, you ask for help from a professional. The other thing you do is draw a line between nature (what carried on down your generation), nurture (how you were raised), and now (what you will do with it).

You are basically saying STOP, to the way your current behavior reflects learned communication and patterns of the past. Difficult, yes? Undoable, no!

Let's start with nurture. Maybe you grew up in a household where you didn't feel safe expressing emotions. Specifically, emotions and feelings around fear. A predictable path later in life is for you to shy away from situations and avoid exposing yourself to anything that you can't control. Why? Because you don't feel comfortable saying "No" in those situations or you don't trust that your feelings will be taken into consideration.

For the men, you probably have a story or two like this. A story that made you feel like crying is unacceptable behavior, or a story that taught you it is best to suffer in silence.

Growing up without being taught how to navigate emotions creates a void. First a linguistic one and then an emotional deficit akin to not learning a language in childhood.

Remember this. It would be unfair to berate yourself for not speaking Spanish if it wasn't part of your early upbringing, so how can you expect yourself to understand how to express emotions in a healthy way when it wasn't modeled for you? In other words, struggling to identify and express emotions later in life is likely a lack of skill in a certain type of language, 'emotional language'.

Acknowledging this is the first step toward learning and healing. It's about recognizing, "Maybe I wasn't taught this; perhaps it wasn't allowed, and that wasn't my fault." Embracing this awareness signifies a reset button, an opportunity to unlearn and relearn healthier emotional expressions.

If you are a man who identifies with a limited number of emotions, I invite you to explore when that range was created. It's very likely that as a child, you never learned how to identify your feelings or felt safe to express those thoughts, feelings, and emotions you are struggling with now. Maybe you were even taught that to have them 'made you weak' or was 'unacceptable.'

Now, that's not a 'get-out-of-jail-free card,' but it is an invitation to dig deeper, read books (well hey you are already doing that now, I honor you for that!), watch videos on YouTube, maybe start counseling and learn more about how to connect with your thoughts, feelings, and emotions. And then to express those in a healthy and effective way.

We can't break out of a prison until we realize we are in one. Generational trauma can act as that emotional, behavioral, or communicational prison that we don't have a conscious awareness we are in!

The last thought I want to leave you with in this chapter is to verbalize the process. You know that what you are working with isn't entirely your fault. As you also know, you will need to hit a reset button and walk a fair bit until you get to healing that part. During that process, you can say to your partner, spouse, friends, or family that you are actively working on this. Try this, "Hey, I know I haven't been doing such a good job with this, but I'm taking steps toward learning. I ask for grace as I go through this process of learning how to express my thoughts, feelings, and emotions. Because for so long, I was made to believe it wasn't okay to even have them."

I'm Becoming My Father & Unbecoming My Father

If I had a nickel every time I heard men say, "I'm acting like my father", I would be a rich man. This wouldn't be so bad if that phrase was meant positively, but almost always, it is not.

When that phrase is said inside the therapy office, it is often accompanied by guilt and shame. It is a realization that the nurture part of the equation, that we discussed before, is now playing out a non-serving and deleterious role in their behavior and circumstances.

The second phrase that is almost always used next is, "I swore I never wanted to be like him." It is such a relief but also a burden to break free from when individuals become aware of this fact.

Conscious recognition is key to understanding patterns of behavior, but it is only the first step. Understanding the negative impact, with an absence of tools to change, still keeps someone in the same cycle.

The next step is where the shift begins. This is when the individual starts to identify, confront, and rewire many of these aspects that mirror how their fathers or caretakers treated them as children. While this realization can be distressing, it's a pivotal moment. This discomfort can catalyze change. It's a point where we can deeply explore our upbringing, understand learned behavior patterns, and question if they align with our desired path.

I've never had a man in counseling express a desire to continue these patterns. Instead, they seek guidance on breaking free from them. This becomes an inflection point, an opportunity for a breakthrough, allowing us to delve into the reasons behind these behaviors without excusing them.

Understanding where these patterns originated fosters compassion for our fathers' or caretakers' struggles. We don't have to excuse or downplay the behavior, but we can demystify it. Once that is done, we see that *who we were as children* had very little effect on *their actions*. They didn't withhold affection or hide their feelings because we didn't deserve it. They did it because they hadn't dealt with their issues, and their fathers had not dealt with their issues, and so on and so on. Once we understand that it was out of our control, we can take responsibility for how we carry that or whether we will continue to do so. In essence, it frees us from carrying their emotional burdens. It's a moment of liberation where we realize these burdens weren't ours to carry, allowing us to heal and forge a new path.

It's also important to note that the absence of having any male role model in our lives can be an aspect of generational trauma. 'Not having' can be just as negatively impactful as having something unhealthy. Having a conscious awareness of how this absence has impacted us and impacted our family tree, is critical to breaking free from generational trauma and making healthy and positive changes in our life.

These moments of awareness are the chain breakers of generational trauma. These moments transform guilt and shame into opportunities for growth and self-realization. They empower us to take accountability for inherited behaviors while consciously deciding what kind of man we want to be and show up as. Embracing these realizations about becoming (or not) like our fathers becomes an essential step toward personal growth and healing.

Actionable Steps

1. **Self-Compassion**
   - Practice self-kindness. Acknowledge the unlearned aspects without self-criticism.

2. **Seek Knowledge**
   - Delve into resources about emotional intelligence and communication.

3. **Counseling or Therapy**
   - Consider professional help to navigate emotional landscapes.

4. **Open Dialogue**
   - Engage in honest conversations with loved ones about your journey.

5. **Establish Boundaries**
   - Recognize where you are sabotaged from practicing the skills and strategies you have learned. Set healthy boundaries in relationships with parents, caregivers, or siblings that perpetuate harmful communication or behavior patterns.

6. **Communication Skills Training**
   - Check out communication workshops or programs that create space for practicing the new communication skills you will learn in this book.

7. **Role Models and Support Networks**
   - Take a very close look at the role models you have in life. Intentionally spend time with people who live by these values and model healthy behavior.

Remember, this isn't about blame; it's about understanding and, ultimately, about the courage to change and grow.

Counseling Perspective on Working with Men

Working as a counselor has afforded me a unique, 'behind-the-scenes' perspective on individuals—both men and women—and the intricacies of the human experience. I engage with people daily, primarily in virtual settings, though I've found myself naturally slipping into my 'counselor role' even in personal interactions with those I encounter on a day-to-day basis.

Those who open up and grant me their trust and vulnerability, share some of their deepest thoughts, feelings, and emotions, and I thank them for that.

While I work with both men and women, a substantial part of my practice involves working with men. I also work with couples, which I'll delve into further in another chapter. However, my focus here is on what I've learned and uncovered through my work with men. While I acknowledge that my insights are based on a relatively small practice size and I don't intend to overgeneralize, there are clear trends.

As a mental health professional, I adhere to ethical and professional boundaries, limiting the sharing of personal anecdotes in sessions. At the same time, I believe that acknowledging my humanness and being vulnerable, helps them know that even professionals 'don't have everything figured out.'

Big Boys Do Cry

I'm not flawless in executing the skills, strategies, and mindset frameworks I teach others. You can see this while reading this book.

The trends that I have noticed in working with men, both personally and professionally, have been quite profound. The first is that men are beginning to let their thoughts, feelings, and emotions surface in a way that can no longer be suppressed. These thoughts, feelings, and emotions were perhaps previously known to conscious awareness and then consciously suppressed, or, more likely, the man was not even consciously aware of them and subconsciously suppressed them. Whatever the case may be, what I have found is that these thoughts, feelings, and emotions are now consciously being brought to the surface in such an incredibly profound way that men are being uncomfortably pressed to recognize them. They are also being invited to make a conscious decision. Are they ready to lean into and unpack the past and the pain, which are often overwhelming and scary, or will they continue to suppress them?

My perspective may be a little biased as a helper and a life-change facilitator. Very often, the individuals who come to me are seeking to lean into and unpack these thoughts, feelings, and emotions. Perhaps, to some extent, they already have. I am sure some men have made the conscious decision to push these thoughts, feelings, and emotions back down. If you, as the reader, are one of those men, there is a choice you can make.

First, you can decide to lean into what's coming up and allow yourself to feel it so that it can be healed. Another option is to consciously push the whole mess of emotions back down. I honor your decision either way. But, if you're reading this book, I believe there's at least some part of you that would like to bring a resolution to what's been stuffed down for so long.

I've witnessed and lived through the struggle to transition from a logical mind to an emotionally open heart. I am here to encourage and support the transition. However, you have free will and autonomy as an individual to decide when or if that will be. And when you find the time is right for you, I invite you to come back to this book. I can tell you that the men I work with who allow themselves to connect to their pain, have a marked shift in their life. It does not happen overnight, but they share with me, and I see in them, how beautiful, more magical, more joyful, and, in many ways, more peaceful their lives become after engaging in counseling.

I want to re-emphasize a crucial point from the start of the book:

Holding it all in isn't what makes you tough.

Holding it all inside is a big part of what makes life tough.

When I'm sitting on the opposite chair (or screen) of men that I work with in my professional practice and watch them struggle with the blockages and internal pressures of a logical mind and an untrained emotionally vulnerable muscle, I tell them "It's okay, man. Let it out". Sometimes we move through this process quite slowly. Because an untrained muscle can't take too much weight too soon. Gentle encouragement, mixed with self-awareness and self-compassion, is the best way to start. When we get it right and the fog lifts and the healing starts and the tears flow, it is a profound, humbling, and magical experience to witness.

Now, for those men who have decided it's time, and that burying things inside is no longer the conscious choice, let's explore together what may come up for you. Fundamentally, as human beings, we all share some basic needs: the desire to be seen, heard, loved, cared about, believed in, and to feel as though we belong. In my work with men, I have observed some major challenges relative to not receiving those needs, which goes back to childhood.

The relationships and experiences during childhood, particularly with primary caregivers, create a profound impact on individuals throughout their adult lives. I define these impacts as the creation of mental programs, akin to the Hindu concept of samskaras or the cognitive behavioral therapy concept of negative schema and cognitive distortions.

These mental programs develop during childhood, especially between zero and seven years old, a period when our brains are mostly in the theta state, absorbing knowledge and understanding about the world and our view of ourselves from our observations and interactions with the outside world. While the human brain has the ability of neuroplasticity and can evolve, a significant portion of this programming occurs in early childhood and adolescence. Interactions with primary caregivers during this time have a monumental influence on how we interact with others as adults.

These mental programs persist until we consciously identify, confront, and rewire them. To do this, we must determine the non-serving programs, identify the ones we want to keep (or at least the ones we don't want to keep), and then rewire our brains with programs that serve us, fostering more loving, compassionate, empathetic, and meaningful relationships with others, especially those closest to us.

In the work I do with men, I often find that their relationship with their primary caregiver, especially if it was their father, involved setting high expectations about what the individual needed to do as a little boy to feel he was deserving of being loved. (**P.S. You didn't need to 'do' anything to be deserving of love!**) Whether it was earning perfect grades, performing chores flawlessly without being asked, or excelling in sports, failure to meet these expectations often resulted in punishment, dismissal, or feelings of inadequacy.

Boys who grew up with these expectations may, as men later in life, put immense pressure on themselves to achieve perfection, denying themselves empathy or compassion when they fall short. This learned behavior gets projected onto their wives, kids, and immediate family, creating household tension and unrealistic expectations.

• • •

Perfection becomes an unrealistic target, constantly moved or reset based on the individual's mood or expectations. These pressures, if not addressed, can lead to deleterious impacts on mental, emotional, and even physical health. While physical health is outside my scope of practice as a mental health professional, my decade of experience in the fitness industry has taught me about its interconnectedness with mental well-being. The pressure and expectations learned in childhood often get projected outward, affecting the mental health of not just the man but also his immediate family.

This brings us back to the choice—whether to lean into the emerging thoughts and emotions or to consciously push them back down. Regardless of your decision, remember that hope and healing are possible. I encourage you to explore your emotions, learn healthier ways to express your thoughts, and strive for vulnerability in your relationships. Whether now is your time or you come back to this book later, the journey toward understanding and healing is yours to embark on.

The Mask

The concept of the mask is found deeply in our cultural ideals, particularly within Western notions of masculinity.

The 'mask,' if you will, is the program that men must appear to wear and operate within. It usually includes an embodiment of toughness, an unyielding persona—a warrior who navigates life's challenges without flinching. And yes, there are moments where such resilience is necessary, where protection becomes a primal instinct for oneself or one's family.

But the mask doesn't understand this nuance and thinks it needs to be on all the time. This is where the struggle is.

When the mask becomes the only face we show to the world, it distorts the natural balance of masculinity, hijacking what's divine about it. The archetype of the hardened warrior, while important in its own right, shouldn't be the entirety of a man's existence.

Constantly wearing this facade of strength becomes exhausting, not to mention, it traps emotions that should be and need to be expressed and resolved.

An additional facet to consider is the role of media and cultural representations in reinforcing these stereotypes.

How many movies, television shows, and books portray men as either hyper-alpha male, or emotionally dead? I'm serious, think about it. We can laugh and say it is just movies, but the effect they have lingers deeply.

This societal insistence on the image of the stoic, emotionless man is based on a false belief: that vulnerability, especially crying, is synonymous with weakness and will diminish one's masculinity.

I want to be clear that most men are unaware they are wearing a mask. I was unaware for a very long time myself. Similarly, those of us who enable the mask (society, partners, friends) are equally unaware we are propagating the mask problem. It is like we keep pushing around the same old opinions, without stopping to think where they come from.

For me, having lived both behind the mask and without it, it is evident that the latter leads to a healthier and more fulfilling life.

The problem with this male archetype lies in its rigidity. It also creates a false sense of power that ignores emotional intelligence, growth, and the vital role of connection.

By demonizing vulnerability, this energy becomes toxic, trapping men in a cycle of emotional ignorance, and preventing them from fully experiencing and understanding their emotions.

Moreover, some toxic partners may inadvertently perpetuate these traits, having been shaped by toxic family environments themselves. This creates an even worse dynamic between couples, with both parties stuck in a cycle that both of them enable. These partners may subconsciously encourage these hardened traits, believing it to be a sign of strength.

Consider a scenario where a woman has grown up in a family environment where emotions are dismissed or suppressed. As a result, she became a nurturing and people-pleasing type of individual.

In her upbringing, she witnessed her male family members being praised for their stoicism, and emotional restraint. She now associates these traits with strength and resilience. She also saw female caregivers allow for that behavior and vent about it with their girlfriends, rather than attempting to change it by having direct conversations with their male partners about what is acceptable and what isn't.

Big Boys Do Cry

When that woman enters into a relationship with a man, she may unknowingly expect him to embody similar characteristics. She also has emotional needs that she hopes to fulfill in the relationship, as all of us do. The woman starts conversations with her partner about her feelings and emotions, but she half-expects them to be shut down, based on previous experience. When her partner is dismissive or avoids emotional topics, the woman may sulk, be upset, or disconnect, but she doesn't feel safe to probe her man at a deeper level about this behavior.

These matchups are pretty common nowadays in our society, where emotionally masked men and fearful, people-pleasing women find themselves in a tango of toxic behaviors.

Neither the woman nor the man are operating from a place of centered and grounded Divine Feminine or Divine Masculine energy.

The other aspect that is worth discussing is the psychological impact the mask can have on men who are somewhat aware. There are a lot of men that know they are putting on this mask for show, but still do it. These men have internalized societal expectations and are experiencing real mental health issues as a result. This can manifest as increased stress, anxiety, angry outbursts, and even depression.

The concept of Divine Feminine and Divine Masculine that I briefly mentioned above is fascinating and worth exploring more.

It isn't about reinforcing traditional gender roles; it's about embracing and balancing the feminine and masculine energies within us all. That energy has power, that we can learn to channel accordingly. Divine Feminine energy embodies qualities such as nurture, compassion, intuition, and emotional depth. On the other hand, Divine Masculine energy embraces strength, leadership, and the ability to protect and promote logic and balance.

Unpacking these concepts is so important if we want to understand how toxic societal norms influence our relationships and wreak havoc. You are not entirely at fault, but you need to do something about it.

For a longer discussion on the Divine Feminine and Divine Masculine, you can turn to the last chapter of this book (Bonus Chapter).

Actionable Steps

1. **Journal and reflect on these questions:**
    - When have I felt pressured to fit into society's idea of what it means to be a man?
    - What emotions do I typically suppress or hide to fit the "male archetype"?
    - Who were the male figures or characters I admired growing up? Do they align with traditional masculinity? Do I still consider them role models?
    - Have I experienced situations where I've avoided showing vulnerability? What are these situations? What do they have in common?

The Physiology of Crying

I am about to change the way you view crying, forever! But to do that, we will have to travel back in time, when we were just babies.

Every pediatrician or health care professional will tell you that ALL healthy babies cry.

So in that regard, everybody has cried at least once.

The first cry shows that your lungs are working. Not crying usually indicates a non-breathing baby or a baby in distress. That doesn't mean all non-crying at-birth babies will have long-term side effects. But it definitely means that a doctor not investigating the cause of the non-crying equals medical malpractice. That is to say, crying is the norm and a lack of that standard response requires immediate attention.

That initial cry is an announcement that all systems are working, especially the respiratory system. How fascinating to think of crying that way - as a universally understood signal for life's commencement.

Let's take a second to unpack that.

First, there is one bit of information that I failed to mention. Babies cry inside the womb. That's right! The mechanism for crying is developed around 20-28 weeks of gestation. This means that even if you didn't cry at birth, you probably cried before that. But why?

Why have we as a species developed the mechanism of crying?

And why does our body continue to use that mechanism?

As with most of the mechanisms of our body that we don't directly control, there must be a function there that serves us and whose purpose is essential to our survival.

That purpose is of course multifaceted, but it starts and ends with bonding.

Consider for a moment the myriad cultural rituals surrounding crying. From mourning ceremonies to joyful crying during celebrations, it serves as a vessel for shared emotions. It brings individuals together in moments of vulnerability and authenticity. It is a universal language.

If we approach crying from the lens of a bonding mechanism, a whole new perspective opens up.

It's not just about the tears themselves, but the emotional bridge they create between individuals. Whether it's a baby crying for nourishment and comfort or adults shedding tears of empathy or relief, the core thread is human connection.

Now, let's talk about tears.

Tears aren't uniform. They manifest in three different forms: basal, reflex, and emotional tears.

Basal tears keep your eyes moist, reflex tears shield against irritants, but what about emotional tears? They are the ones triggered by intense feelings, be it joy, sorrow, or relief. But... surprise! They are not just about emotions. The last category of tears packs a hormonal punch too.

They can boost cortisol, the stress hormone, while also adding higher levels of endorphins, your body's natural pain relief, giving you a mood upgrade.

It helps to think of crying as the body's valve for emotional pressure. (life is better when we are proactive about using this valve!) It lets out stress, tension, and even toxins, making you feel instantly refreshed. Plus, it's not just in your head; it's physiological too.

Big Boys Do Cry

Your body's autonomic nervous system is no stranger to tears. During stress, the sympathetic nervous system revs up, raising your heart rate and breathing. This is where crying enters the arena, like a calming agent, bringing your body back to Zen energy mode.

Have you ever noticed how your breath syncs with tears when you cry? That's no fluke. Crying and breathing work together, calming your emotions. It's that deep, rhythmic breathing, a natural response to inner turmoil, that brings in more oxygen, leveling things out.

And here's the brain twist. Crying isn't just about the tears. It sparks the production of oxytocin and endorphins, the feel-good neurotransmitters, making you feel connected and understood when you cry in front of others.

Now, shifting gears back to the little ones. A baby's cry isn't just a signal for milk. It's the superhero signal for the "milk let-down reflex." It's the call for nourishment, triggering a love-filled response in mom's body. Mom hears her baby crying. Involuntarily, breast milk starts to flow.

That cry-milk connection? It's not just about the feeding. There's a whole emotional tango going on. It's the dance between a baby's cry, the comforting milk, and the love that forms an unbreakable bond between mother and child.

Nature is genius that way. Now let's recap.

Crying kicks off our journey in this world. It's a sign of life, indicating healthy breathing in a newborn. Yet, as we grow, the narrative around crying shifts. Somehow, it becomes a sign of weakness, particularly for men. We're taught to hold back tears, to cry in private, or even worse, to NOT cry at all.

But here's the twist: crying isn't a sign of weakness. It's an essential part of healthy communication. Babies cry to signal their needs, and that communication continues throughout life. When we stop or suppress our tears, we lose a crucial aspect of expressing our emotions.

If we examine relationships between women, we see this unwritten pact in action—crying in front of each other is normal. They create a space for these emotions, understanding that it's a way to communicate feelings and connect on a deeper level. They validate each other's emotions through tears.

However, for men, crying in front of others, let alone their partners, can feel like crossing a line. This could not be further from the truth. Don't let anybody tell you otherwise. Crying in front of your partner can be transformative. It shows vulnerability, trust, and a willingness to be emotionally open. It breaks down the barriers that hinder genuine connection.

When a man cries with or in front of his partner, it's not a sign of weakness; it's a display of trust and emotional intelligence. It allows for a deeper understanding and communication.

In my own life, I've experienced the power of crying in front of my wife. But let's not forget, I wasn't always this way. It was a pivotal moment that shifted the dynamics of our relationship. Later on, I'll share how my wife's response to seeing me cry became one of the most impactful moments in our journey together.

Her response to my tears wasn't judgment or discomfort; it was understanding, compassion, and acceptance. And here is the catch - even though I had seen women behave this way towards each other and even though I had witnessed previous partners open the door for me to claim that space of vulnerability for myself, I rarely if ever chose to walk through it.

If you take a close look at the relationship with your partner, and if your partner is someone you admire, value, and respect, something tells me you will find that door open for you as well.

The women in our lives often wait for us to walk through it, setting the stage and inviting us in.

Like the person who jumps into the water first and yells out, "The water is fine, come on in!".

Actionable Steps

1. **Acknowledge your perspective on crying.**
   - Do you view crying as a negative emotion or one reserved for you in private? Unpack it!

2. **Recognize and create safe spaces.**
   - Start to look at the people in your life who have welcomed emotional exchange.
   - Explore that space with someone, or test how it feels to hold that space for someone else while they cry.

3. **Start with communication.**
   - Communicate openly with your partner or friends about emotions that come up.
   - Commit yourself to the ongoing journey of discovery within a space of vulnerability and emotional expression.

Real Men Cry, Together

In earlier chapters, we explored the transformative power of crying, primarily within the context of relationships with partners or spouses. However, there's an aspect seldom broached: the significance of crying among men and how this experience can lead to a profound connection with other men. It's a topic often left untouched.

I've spoken to a lot of men about the moment they first cried in front of their wives, but what about a male friend?

When it comes to shedding tears among peers or other men, the conversation typically fades into silence. There are also a lot of prejudices and stereotypes that enter the discussion fairly quickly.

The defensive mechanism comes up and says, "They won't respect me as much.", "They will think I'm weak.", "I would be bullied or criticized." Even men that have done it and received a positive response back, may feel that they still "lost" something in the process. That something is the mask of the male archetype that we have discussed.

Crying in front of others or with other men is just as important as crying when we are alone.

When we build a wall of defenses around a natural process, we stagnate. I want to be very clear that my advice is not to go find friends and cry with them uncontrollably.

It's intriguing, though, isn't it? We readily share laughs and meals with our friends, cherishing those moments of joy and camaraderie. Yet, when it comes to shedding tears, there's often an unspoken restraint. Why is that? Why do we hold ourselves back from expressing such a raw, fundamental emotion in the company of our friends?

Your friends are safe places where you bring your joy, sorrow, and presence. You trust your friends, you love them, and respect them. If you come across a funny joke while in their company, you will share it. But will you share a moment of weakness? That is a prejudice, or internal blockage, that needs to be unpacked.

Perhaps it's time to question these social conventions and explore the authenticity and depth that emotional vulnerability can bring to our friendships.

I'd like to share a story with you from my college days at the University of Scranton. It was a smaller school, and everyone pretty much knew each other. One of my close friends, Brad, and I met during freshman year. Both of us were athletic guys who'd been into sports and hitting the gym in high school, so we kind of represented the 'macho' freshman guys on campus.

Throughout the semester, we'd cross paths, we wouldn't talk, but there was no animosity between us, just mutual respect. But one night during the winter interim classes, Brad and I ended up running into each other at the same party. We were both a bit tipsy, enough I guess to finally start talking with each other. The next thing I know, we are doing shots from turkey basters – yeah, those big Thanksgiving ones! That moment solidified our friendship, and it's lasted ever since 2004.

That bonding moment was triggered when we let our guards down and got vulnerable. (Alcohol played a part in letting our guards down, and I'm not endorsing it as the doorway to vulnerability, but I want to keep it real with you!) Since that bonding moment during our freshman year, Brad and I have both laughed and cried together. Now, laughing you can do with everyone, but crying, well that is a different kind of connection that doesn't happen with just anyone. We fostered a mutual respect and admiration for each other, which led to an ability to feel safe with each other and to be raw and real with each other.

In another instance at the end of my junior year, there was this other big guy on campus, he was a wrestler, whom Brad and I often saw in the gym. Brad and I were always cordial with him, with no 'bad blood' but up until that point we weren't overly close. He was a senior and getting ready to graduate. This was during the final months of school for the year, and for the seniors, it was that time of the year when people wanted to 'get things off their chests' before graduating. Anyway, he came to my room one night, when Brad and I were drinking before heading to the bar. He sat down, looking a bit uneasy.

Brad and I were having a good time, music blasting, planning to head out, when suddenly, this guy, sitting on the bed, asked me to turn the music off.

I was a bit shocked. (and a bit like dude, don't kill the vibe!)

He started expressing how he'd wanted to be friends with us all along but felt intimidated or unsure of how to connect. There had been this unspoken dynamic throughout our time at school, you know, like an invisible barrier.

And as he poured out his feelings, he started to cry.

It was unexpected, (remember the mask) a big guy like him, crying amidst our party vibes. Yet, something shifted between him, Brad, and me at that moment of his crying. It wasn't animosity we felt. It wasn't a weakness we saw, it was more like a softening, for all of our guards.

I remember at that moment feeling so connected. We all ended up 'hugging it out' and having a really good conversation before going out to the bar. (and hell yes, we turned up the music and did some shots before we left!)

I remember that night like it was yesterday, sitting next to him, offering support, saying, "I'm here for you, man," and from that point onwards,

Big Boys Do Cry

our friendship grew stronger throughout our remaining time at school and even after graduation. To this day, Brad and I have reflected on that moment of vulnerability and how it changed things for the three of us as men.

This is why I want you to understand that crying isn't just about strengthening connections with your partner; it also holds immense power in connecting with other men in your life. As a counselor, I've sat with some incredibly tough men, war veterans, and law enforcement officers, who've been through unimaginable situations. That's why it is so humbling, and I'm so grateful when they can give themselves permission to connect with their feelings and allow themselves to cry in front of me in our counseling work together.

When men, especially those with a tough exterior, allow themselves to be vulnerable and cry, it creates this profound environment for connection that extends to those around us. You see, opening up and being vulnerable and even crying is not just about relationships with partners; it's about forming a deeper bond with fellow men, regardless of your profession or background. Opening up, living from the heart, and communicating on that level creates an incredible level of support and connection.

Actionable Steps

1. **Personal Reflection:**
   - Have I ever held back from showing emotions like crying among my male friends? Why is that?

2. **Friendship Dynamics:**
   - Do I feel safe and comfortable expressing vulnerability with my male friends?
   - Make a list of people you do and don't feel comfortable with and why.

3. Recall Experiences

- Have I ever witnessed or experienced moments of emotional vulnerability among male friends? How did I react at that moment? How do I wish I had reacted?

Left Brain vs Right Brain

Let's take a moment to explore the significant differences between left-brain and right-brain dominance. Keep in mind, these are generalizations and may not apply universally.

To simplify the science behind it: the left brain is associated with logic, problem-solving, and a goal-oriented approach. Many men resonate with this description as it often aligns with their natural thought processes—focused, practical, and solution-driven.

The left brain says, 'I'm going to get things done.'

The right side of the brain is more intuitive.

It is also linked to creativity and an emotional understanding. This intuitive aspect is commonly associated with being in touch with one's emotions, a characteristic often attributed, though not exclusively, to women.

As the adage goes, men tend to be more hardened and closed down, and women are more expressive of their thoughts, feelings, and emotions.

For this, we are going to refer to men as left-brain dominant.

Of course, logic and problem-solving can be a tremendous gift. But staying there for too long can also be very frustrating, both for ourselves and for our wife or partner.

The best option is to find the balance and practice dominance when needed.

To help men move more into the right side of the brain, we can do various things. It can be stimulated while listening to music, drawing, and doing different creative tasks. Talk therapy focused on naming emotions and feelings can also help with this, and it is a substantial part of my clinical work with men.

Of course, let's not forget crying!

When we cry, it's a beautiful thing because we're connected to our hearts and to our emotions. We're not trying to solve problems when we are crying, we are attuned to our emotional state. We're in our hearts, and we are open to connecting with other people's hearts. That is a very right brain-dominant action.

A strategic balance of left and right brain thinking is very important when it comes to couples, since it allows them to explore both sides of a situation or disagreement.

With that in mind, I want to offer a story that places crying within a realm that might be easier to connect with and understand.

It's May 2022. I'm in my home office in Bellingham, Washington, wrapping up the final day of my clinical mental health counseling internship. The emotions hit hard—excitement, happiness, and a profound sense of purpose. Completing this phase marks the end of an intense journey. I managed to condense a three-and-a-half-year program into two years, a significant accomplishment.

After class, I call my wife to catch up on my plans to move to Canada. Amidst the chaos, I unexpectedly start to share about my schooling, realizing it's my last day of class. Suddenly, emotions overwhelm me— I'm crying, unable to articulate the depth of what I feel. All I manage to express is how much this journey means to me, and how grateful and humbled I am. It's a flood of relief and joy, a recognition that my calling, my purpose, aligns with counseling. There was so much craziness going on in my life, but at that moment I was FULLY present and so grateful.

You know what's wild? Men are already tapping into that right-brain vibe, they just don't always realize it. Think about it—when you're jamming out to music, getting lost in a game, or even appreciating a killer piece of art, that's your right brain taking the wheel.

The thing is, sometimes we forget to give credit to that side of ourselves. It's like we overlook it, dismissing it as just fun or entertainment. But in those moments, we're feeling things, embracing emotions, and letting our creative side run free—all classic right-brain moves.

So, it's not like we're totally clueless about it. We just need to remember that it's not all about solving problems and 'being the fixer.' Our right brain is already doing its thing; we just need to give it a high-five and let it out to play more often.

Crying... for the W-I-N

Let's look at another example of how us men can shift into the right side of our brain and not even realize it. We associate crying with sadness, but there's a beautiful aspect rarely acknowledged—the tears shed from being deeply connected to our hearts and passions. It's not just for sadness or grief; it's for joy and love. Those tears symbolize the profound ways our heart speaks to us.

Men often lead with that left side of the brain, emphasizing logic and analysis. Yet, moments like these break through the barriers, transcending the analytical nature, and they are perhaps some of the only 'socially acceptable' situations in which men have been programmed to look at crying as 'ok.'

Can you think of other moments where we are moved to tears through joy or experience what I call a 'duality of crying?'

The best way to explain this duality is sports. Consider for a moment the way we witness our favorite NHL or NFL stars winning a championship and shedding tears. There is no judgment, right?

Even before I delved into exploring my own emotions and healing journey, I never criticized or thought less of professional athletes who cried, whether it was due to winning or losing. It was completely acceptable. Even when they lost, there was no mockery from me or from those whom I watched sports with.

Let's pause and ponder this for a moment, guys. Why is it that we don't judge these superstars crying when they win or lose a major sporting event, yet we were taught since childhood that "big boys don't cry," and that we should toughen up and suppress our emotions?

Why is crying considered unacceptable in other contexts, but when it happens in the realm of sports, particularly during significant wins or losses, it's not only acceptable but almost expected?

Crying doesn't imply weakness; it means we're connected to the core of who we are, to our true essence. It's fascinating, isn't it? In sports, in certain aspects, crying is okay, but in almost all other areas of traditional masculinity, it's frowned upon. I encourage you to challenge yourself, to reflect on this difference.

Would you view Sidney Crosby or LeBron James crying as they hold up the championship trophy differently from Bob crying at work? It's a challenge to examine our perceptions. I'll admit, there was a time in my life when I'd watch athletes cry in sports and think nothing of it. But if a friend cries, it might make me uncomfortable or prompt me to tell them to 'toughen up.' I'm inviting you to explore that distinction within yourself.

Because even though we lead with our left brain a lot of the time, we already can exercise the right side. Sports competitions are an arena where men allow themselves to let go and engage the right side of their brains. Now, you can examine other areas of your life where you can put that skill into action!

Actionable Steps

1. **Understanding my brain**
   - Where do I feel my left brain dominates in everyday situations?
   - Where do I let my right brain take over?
   - In what situations do I apply both problem-solving and intuitive, emotional thinking?

2. **Right brain activation**
   - What creative and emotional activities do I enjoy that I can incorporate into my life?
   - What activities can stimulate my right brain with music, art, and creative tasks?

3. **Reframing crying**
   - Can I recall moments where crying was a response to joy, success, or profound emotions?
   - Did those tears feel different from tears as a response to sadness, or grief?
   - How do I feel when I witness men cry in joyful situations (weddings, births, sports events, promotions)

Vulnerability = Strength

When it comes to strength, I invite you to look at it from a perhaps new, or different way. Try approaching it as an internal journey. Typically, us men associate strength with external prowess, progress, and the ability to forge ahead in projects or physical tasks. Undoubtedly, that demands a remarkable level of strength.

However, in my journey toward healing, I've discovered a different kind of strength—a deeper, more intrinsic one. It stems from the willingness to embark on an inward journey, to confront and explore those complex thoughts, feelings, and emotions that can often feel scary or overwhelming.

Reflecting on my own experiences, I've found that my proudest moments, where I truly felt strong, were when I leaned into those profound and challenging emotions. It takes an incredible amount of courage and strength to confront and explore these inner realms. We all have different challenges and setbacks we have to navigate, but the feelings we get when we face them are quite similar.

As men, such introspection probably wasn't part of our upbringing. How often were we encouraged or taught by our fathers or grandfathers to delve deeply into our emotional landscapes? Growing up did you ever have your grandfather or your dad say to you, "Well son, I just had a really deep emotional experience, let me share with you what I learned."? Such conversations were likely rare within our social circles or relationships, even as adults.

Big Boys Do Cry

I want to emphasize this point, hoping this book can serve as a catalyst for a shift in perspective. Yes, as men, we exhibit strength outwardly, but there's an overlooked aspect—an inner strength. This form of strength, I believe, truly reflects our depth and resilience. It lies in our ability to connect with our emotions and sit with them, uncovering their roots.

That, in essence, is genuine strength—an inward journey and one that has a key ingredient: vulnerability.

David Meltzer frames it brilliantly: "When I am vulnerable, I actually become invulnerable." When I embrace vulnerability, I break free from the confines of my ego and the limiting mental scripts. When I'm vulnerable I live from my heart. I'm not trapped in non-serving mental programs. Instead of fearing hurt or guarding against potential harm, vulnerability empowers me.

If you've ever seen the biographical movie '8 Mile' which features rap star Eminem, there is a part in the movie where he has a battle with another rapper. But Eminem does something unique, he raps about all of his flaws, thereby disabling the other rapper from being able to make fun of him. This is another way of describing the power of vulnerability and how it makes us invulnerable.

After my arrest in 2013, worry and fear clouded my job interviews. Questions about my past arrest left me feeling like a failure as I struggled to secure a new job afterward. I had to shift my approach. Instead of waiting for people to bring up my arrest (which made my heart sink in fear), I brought it up first.

I made the decision that I would go into the interviews and say, "Let me tell you what makes me unique. I was arrested, and I hit rock bottom of rock bottoms. Everything that I thought meant the world to me at that time was taken. And now let me tell you what I learned from that. Let me tell you how I grew from that."

The new approach was telling my story with vulnerability. I was humble but confident. I could sit outside the shame and present the person I truly was. The person that had grown immensely, and had picked himself back up from rock bottom.

With that mindset, everything shifted at once.

The idea that being vulnerable is a tremendous strength goes against so much of what we are taught in life. We think being strong equals being tough or having your guard up. But holding a shield at all times is a sign of weakness.

Now, you might think, "But Ryan, there are times when we need to have our guards up, right?". To that, I say YES! There is a balance between advocating for yourself, advocating for your family, and being strong. There is also a time for connecting with people, knowing how to speak from the heart, and living life from the heart.

When we can harness both of those energies, life starts to get very good.

Before diving in further, let's make a distinction. Vulnerability is strength, yes! But it isn't emotional dumping.

You don't come home and unload all negative emotions to your partner as a form of vulnerability.

Vulnerability means being connected to our hearts. When we do that, we can speak and communicate from our hearts to create a connection with our spouse, partner, or friend.

Vulnerability creates bonds, it doesn't break them down. It does that through shared experiences, acknowledging our universal human emotions—pain, joy, fear, just to name a few. By sharing our stories, we foster understanding and connection. We bridge the gaps between us and allow the other person to truly see us. It also helps them feel safe to show their true self to us.

Big Boys Do Cry

We're all human and we all have much more in common than we think. We all experience pain, we've all likely experienced grief, and we've all hopefully experienced joy and happiness.

When vulnerability 'enters the chat,' it builds a connecting thread between those shared feelings of the human experience. Not because it wants to project it onto somebody, but because in doing so it facilitates and enhances connection.

Another example at the front of my mind when thinking of vulnerability as strength goes back to my travel hockey days. When cancer struck our coach, all of us in the team showed our support by shaving our heads.

I distinctly remember the day Coach Connelly shared his diagnosis. He walked into our locker room, vulnerable, teary-eyed and took off his hat to reveal his chemotherapy induced bald head. It was a moment that has always stuck with me. Until then, I hadn't seen a bunch of guys come together like that. Witnessing Coach's vulnerability and strength, and our team uniting to support him, sparked something in me about the power of vulnerability and shedding tears.

Men often link vulnerability and crying with weakness, but that's far from the truth. It takes courage to show vulnerability, to shed tears, and to stand by it. It's saying, "I'm confident in who I am, and I'm okay showing my emotions authentically."

As individuals, especially as leaders, being authentic and willing to cry doesn't diminish our strength. Instead, it shows that we're true to ourselves. That we aren't afraid to be real. Whether it's at work, with a team, or in a community, being real and embracing emotions can inspire courage and strength in others.

So, here's a reminder: don't shy away from living authentically. You're human, entitled to a range of emotions. You can cry, laugh, and love – that's the human experience. Embracing this authenticity might surprise

• • •

you and even inspire others around you. It's about being a man but also being true to the human you are.

Vulnerability = Safety

Now what about safety?

We have discussed vulnerability in a number of different ways and through different frameworks.

Now, I invite you to think of vulnerability as a meeting ground for safety.

Safety is what facilitates the environment for *communication.*

Communication is what builds *connection.*

And the more *connected* we are, the deeper we can give and receive *love.*

Imagine this scenario: I approach John, and rather than pushing him to open up about his recent breakup, I vulnerably share a story of my heartbreak. By doing so, I create a safe space for him to share his emotions too. While speaking to John, I bring up the time my first girlfriend broke up with me back in high school. I share how she was the reason I got into working out, and how it helped me overcome the feelings of "forever and always" that I had envisioned. Contrast that with approaching John and demanding he "toughen up" and telling him to 'get over it and move on.'

Which of those approaches is more likely to get John to open up and tell me how I can best support him?

When we *lead with vulnerability* in those moments, we open the door for the other person to do the same.

Now, consider intimate relationships. If I openly express my feelings of loneliness to my wife and link it to my childhood experiences, acknowledging it's not about her, it cultivates an environment of safety and understanding. But if I react defensively or with blame, it doesn't foster a safe space for her to engage.

Sadly, as men, our default response often leans toward stoicism, which isn't conducive to creating safety. Women, on the other hand, thrive on feeling secure enough to communicate deeply.

Vulnerability initiates safety, which then fuels healthy communication. I witness this frequently in my work with couples. When both parties are stuck in their triggers and not feeling safe, communication stalls. Nobody is feeling seen or heard. To tie this all together, if the atmosphere lacks safety, effective communication and conflict resolution become very hard. But if we intentionally check for and attempt to create vulnerable and emotionally safe moments, there is a foundation for genuine connection, healing, and love.

Actionable Steps

1. **Reflect and journal on these questions:**
   - Have I ever felt strong when I've opened up about my emotions or been vulnerable with others?
   - How do I define strength within myself? Is it linked to my external abilities or my willingness to express emotions?
   - When was the last time I felt shame when showing vulnerability?

2. **Leading by example**
   - How can I find safe places to express my emotions vulnerably?
   - Can I remember a moment where my defensiveness and inability to be vulnerable led to a negative outcome?

Exploring Specific Emotions

Recently I found myself on two different mountains within less than 24 hours.

I have always loved the mountains. Maybe it is being outdoors, or maybe it is the feeling you get when you overcome a challenge. Going up and up, then eventually coming down and thinking about the journey. As I had a moment to reflect, I thought about the emotional buildup within men.

See, it's like being on a gondola, gradually ascending to the mountaintop. You're taking in and being exposed to a variety of experiences, feeling the emotions rise, layer by layer, just like the pressures building inside a volcano, each layer contributing to the mounting tension. The peak moments? Those happen in the thick of arguments, the volcanic eruptions of emotions.

Most of the individuals I work with will experience this gradual buildup of emotions, as though going up a mountain. It's not an immediate eruption but rather a gradual accumulation. It is like a volcano building up steam.

And if we pay attention, we see moments where the volcano is ready to burst and moments where it is slowly but steadily building up that steam.

Can we prevent the proverbial volcano from erupting? Sure!

At the surface level, the main power that fuels the volcano is anger. Other culprits are feeling unappreciated, defeated, tired, exhausted, emasculated, diminished and disrespected.

• • •

One or two of these now and then are not bad. As we said, it's part of the human experience. Non-serving or negative emotions can reveal what we need to work on. They may also highlight patterns of behavior that we refuse to let go of.

But when there is a consistent fueling of the pressure and no way to offload any of them, then disaster strikes. A volcanic eruption might not annihilate the surrounding area immediately, but over time, with enough explosions, none of the land will be good for cultivation.

The ash will settle in thick layers and prevent water, and nourishment from going into the soil. Anything trapped in the explosion will remain unchanged for years to come.

What helps us avoid the volcano like build up of pressure and prevent an explosion?

Exercise, time in nature, and therapy, just to name a few. By engaging in these activities, we allow and create spaces that facilitate an outpouring of emotions in a healthy way. It is a judgment-free zone, where we not only lift the cap and let off steam, but we also examine the steam and understand it so it doesn't go back in straight away.

When we are dealing with pressure that has been building up for years and years, therapy is a great option.

With that initial outburst examined, you can begin to practice ways to let go of the steam gradually during everyday life.

I Feel Angry

In my work with men, anger emerges as one of the most prevalent emotions.

I've come to define anger as a manifestation of repressed and unexpressed emotions. This means that while it may come up as anger, it is often not what the stored emotion was originally. It could be stored frustration, a sense of being unseen, unrecognized, or unappreciated.

That initial negative emotion is stored, rather than expressed.

To give you a better example, consider this.

You are arguing with your wife or partner when out of nowhere, she is accusing you of being unreasonable and illogical. You are triggered. Your anger is rising and you find yourself behaving in ways you know you shouldn't.

Both of you want to solve this but can't. She sees the situation one way and you see it another way. You may be angry about the situation at hand, but what's underneath that anger?

Think about sitting in an outdoor hot tub on a freezing winter's day. You are relaxing and the sun is glistening all around you. As you begin to pay attention, you see the sun catching the steam. Our emotions may be likened to that steam. The steam comes from the hot water beneath, but it's in a different form. We may see that steam expressed as anger, but what I've come to uncover in my work with men as a counselor is that the water, the very root of the anger, is often quite different.

The water is the suppressed and stored emotion. The steam is a by-product of the stored emotion.

This is why it is so important to focus on the stored patterns of emotions, the source of the steam, rather than only on the steam itself.

You might even think it is healthy not to express your feelings and suppress the trigger, without communicating it to your wife, or partner. This internal dialogue could sound something like " Man, it's just not worth it to bring this up" or, "She won't listen." Or maybe you don't even recognize the difference between the steam and the water. At least not at a conscious level.

Nevertheless, this internalized anger eventually explodes outward, an eruption of pent-up energy release.

Interestingly, beneath this seemingly overwhelming anger could lie layers of emotions. Loneliness might be one of them, subtly veiled by this outward display of frustration. For men navigating these emotions, I encourage the acknowledgment and expression of these thoughts and feelings.

You see, there's no such thing as pushing it aside; it's only pushing it further inside.

And that's detrimental to our well-being.

I don't care who we are, man or woman. And for the wives and partners out there reading this book, I would invite you to perhaps use this framework as well when these emotions come up. Ask yourself; What's underneath my anger?

Engage with your partner, not just about the anger they display but inquire gently about what lies beneath it. It's a two-way street for both men and women, though, in my work, I've observed this pattern of anger significantly among men.

To facilitate healing and deeper connections in relationships, it's essential to unearth the root cause of this anger. Men, when you sense anger bubbling up, it's crucial to introspect. Ask yourself: What's the trigger behind this surge of emotion? Is it truly about the laundry on the couch, or does it reflect a deeper sense of feeling unacknowledged or unappreciated in certain aspects of life?

Maybe it's been an accumulation of instances that went unnoticed, fostering a sense of underappreciation over time. These unspoken feelings, when bottled up, can culminate in an explosive burst of anger. Reflecting on these triggers can unravel powerful insights into our emotional landscapes.

The other reason why anger becomes a go-to emotion for many guys is because it fits in so well with the Male Archetype and the unhealthy expressions of hyper-masculinity.

The masculine energy inside wants to be a protector and a leader. When left unchecked, it goes into overdrive and becomes over dominant. I say "over dominant" because that's the thing—masculine energy is meant to be assertive, to have your back and protect your loved ones, radiating confidence. However, when it goes too far unchecked, it can turn into a controlling vibe. That assertiveness turns into aggressiveness, and that can easily spiral into anger.

The real mess and trickiness start when this aggressiveness takes over. See, most of us weren't taught how to tap into our heart space, to figure out our emotions and healthily express them. We've been wired to believe that if being assertive doesn't cut it, you've got to get aggressive, and if that doesn't work, it's time to get angry. It's like a flawed road map—we've only been shown one path, even if it's full of potholes and pitfalls.

Think about it like this: if you were never shown an alternative route, you'd stick to what you know, right? That's why so many of us guys get caught in this cycle—from being assertive to aggressive to boiling over in anger. Few of us ever had a conversation growing up that said, "Hey, there are other ways to communicate your needs." We probably didn't see men around us using anything other than anger when they felt their needs weren't met.

It's like a mix of nature and nurture. Some of it's wired into us, while some of it is learned behavior. The lack of exposure to any other form of expression, along with the natural tendencies of masculine energy, has driven many of us to think that the only way to get what we need is through this assertiveness-aggressiveness-anger route.

The paradox here is that once you get to anger, you are living in a place of fear and powerlessness. So, all the healthy levels of masculine energy you wanted are completely out of balance.

This toxic byproduct, commonly known as 'toxic masculinity', is, in my opinion, a reflection of our deepest weakness as men. We feel powerless, so we go into overdrive with the tool we inherently know best.

There's a fine line here, though. Sure, a healthy dose of assertiveness or dominance in a relationship is good and can be warmly received by our partner. Because the woman in our life and that Divine Feminine, is looking to be protected and so very much wants to feel safe in the strength of her male partner. But too much of it, an overdose, can turn toxic for the relationship. It all boils down to the lack of connection to our emotions—our heart space.

Now, don't get me wrong. I'm not saying this is how it is for everyone. But from my own experiences and those of the guys I know and work with, it was pretty common not to witness vulnerability or heartfelt communication as a way to fulfill needs.

Remember, there's a whole range of communication beyond this assertive-aggressive-angry loop that many of us got stuck in and it is waiting for you to use it.

I Feel Pressured

Time to talk about pressure as it relates to men.

There is good pressure and bad pressure. Good pressure is what shapes boys into healthy men. We step up in our role as providers, forming a foundation around which a family will thrive. Every single one of us needs a bit of pressure to bring out good qualities. Like a rough diamond needs a chisel.

Ryan Joseph Kopyar

Without pressure, we are nothing but bodies with animal instincts and a brain that can make rationalizations for bad behavior. We don't want that! Good pressure forces us to show up to work, serve our communities, take care of our loved ones, and even create life.

Then there is bad pressure, the type men put on themselves that forces them into toxic or unhealthy patterns and behaviors. This manifests in various ways and it almost always comes up in the work I do with men. I've also felt it in my life - a relentless demand for everything to be flawless, for life to fit into a perfect mold. This is especially common in Western culture, where societal demands are placed on men to be the financial breadwinner for their families.

When we hyperfocus on that, however, we lose out on a lot more.

A provider does not only mean someone who brings food to the table and looks after the finances. It's also not just about being the protector.

Being there for our loved ones transcends the realm of finances and protection. It is about showing up emotionally, being there for our children, and offering love, presence, and understanding.

How do you change it then? The message I'd like to convey here is to ease up a bit. It is time to shift the value you place on yourself from being just a financial provider to being a present, loving, flawed but ultimately whole individual.

This is a beautiful gift to yourself and your loved ones. Your presence, your love, and your wholeness hold value that no dollar amount can compare to. When you feel that tug to put in those extra work hours or pick up additional shifts, take a moment to consider: perhaps what your family truly needs from you as a man is not just the financial support, but your presence, your affection, and your heartfelt connection.

To do that you will have to break down the conditioning that led you here. But the reward will be so much greater.

I Feel Wronged

Have you ever heard the phrase "resentment is the silent killer of relationships"?

If I could make a Top 5 list of the most destructive emotions that break down relationships, families, and individuals, resentment would be up there.

Resentment is a silent intruder that creeps into moments and turns them into poison.

It sneaks unnoticed at first and settles into the deepest corners of our emotions. It corrupts good energy into ugly, corrosive energy. Men who walk into my office, myself included, have experienced this in buckets.

When you feel wronged by someone else's actions or life's circumstances, it creates fertile ground for a cascade of unhealthy patterns. These patterns when left to grow unchecked grow deep roots that continue to grow.

Feeling wronged is a potent emotion. It colors our interactions with everyone, but especially our partners and children. It also can dictate our responses. It is like a game that has only one ending, yet you are there continuing to play it.

Here's the thing about feeling wronged—it can quickly become a trap. The more we hold onto it, nurturing our sense of injustice, the more it defines our narrative. It begins to shape our reactions, clouding our ability to see beyond our hurt.

If you are already in therapy, you might recognize those reactions in you. You walk into the office, you start listing all the things wrong with your partner, friend, parent, or business associate. You are on the defensive, trying to prove what they did and how they did it. You want to feel validated. You want me to tell you that they did you wrong.

The problem with this is simple. Even if you get that validation you crave at that moment, nothing changes. If you keep holding onto the feeling without expressing it with those who need to hear it and you will keep betraying your true emotions and let the surface-level toxic emotions run amok. The only thing that can grow inside that environment is distrust, defensiveness, and vindictiveness.

Breaking free from this cycle of feeling wronged requires a radical shift—an embrace of vulnerability.

We have already talked about how vulnerability is a strength. So here we are once again confirming this premise. When you find yourself on the defensive, it is time to do something brave: be open and honest.

First, you start with acknowledging your hurt. You express your emotions and seek understanding rather than retaliation. You own your feelings and communicate them even when it feels so very uncomfortable.

Bringing up even just one situation or one emotional feeling that we have, may seem a simple and easy action to take, but I understand it takes a lot of courage. It requires a tremendous willingness to confront your emotions head-on. It involves peeling away layers of hurt and resentment not only as it relates to this situation right here and right now but also to the generational trauma and hurt you are carrying.

You are bringing all your unmet needs, unresolved conflicts, and misunderstood intentions and asking for them to be seen by those closest to you.

I've been called to this uncomfortable meeting ground many times as I'm sure you have too. Not every time did I feel seen or heard. Sometimes, I reverted to leading with anger rather than vulnerability or buried down my feelings, instead of reaching out with truth and honesty. If this happens to you do not be discouraged, these are new tools and skills that you are learning. Heck, even for someone like me who knows many of the skills and tools to use, I can still make mistakes and fall into old patterns. It's part of being human, we're not always going to get it right, but we keep trying with the promise of understanding that holding our thoughts, feelings, and emotions inside and not communicating them is not the healthy solution.

I Feel Unsupported

It's a Saturday morning, and I'm downstairs on my couch watching ESPN College GameDay, enjoying a cup of coffee after a hectic work week. Usually, my wife and I chat while she cooks breakfast for me and the kids. These moments are typically peaceful and joyful, although sometimes the tiredness shows. This Saturday morning ritual has become a time for reflection on the past week and appreciating how hard we have worked and the challenges we have faced.

But this particular Saturday, my anxiety is surging. I bring up my Canadian spousal sponsorship application, feeling the pressure of a tight deadline. As we discuss it, my anxiety grows into frustration, then anger. I start yelling.

Deep down, I feel unsupported and unappreciated.

While she is sharing her feedback on what will happen, and what needs to happen, plus why some of the obstacles are in place, all I feel is let down.

My wife, a paralegal familiar with the process, had promised to help complete the application. She's done 85%, but the remaining 15% is crucial. Despite feeling disappointed about the delay, my anger is unwarranted. She has already done most of it, and I know she cares.

This is no longer a conversation. This is me yelling loud enough that her daughter's friends can hear me from the other room.

● ● ●

Ryan Joseph Kopyar

NOT one of my *proudest moments.*

I have gone from a peaceful Saturday morning to a raging person.

Of course, I have "valid" reasons inside my head. I can't start working in Canada until this certification is completed. This has caused me a lot of stress for months. Every time I cross the border, the Canadian Border Services agents are growing impatient with my incomplete application. My visitor record deadline is approaching in about 90 days, which adds to the pressure.

The application in my head is now this huge aspect of our lives, personally and professionally.

The more she is trying to explain and help me through it, the angrier I get. The angrier I get, the more my wife begins to shut down.

Had I stopped for a second and checked what the feeling under the anger was, I would have said, "feeling unsupported and unappreciated". Maybe I would also have said that I don't feel important enough and that I was projecting onto her the hurt of being let down by people in my past.

In moments like these, we enter what I call childhood territory. For all the grown-up facade of a professional, a man with a wife, and a job and responsibilities, I'm acting like a 3-year-old little boy whose mother never came home. I'm letting my emotions control the narrative inside my head.

My rational brain was trying to tell me to calm down, but my past hurt was saying, "I needed you, you weren't there for me, and I don't understand why."

You see for me, there have been various aspects of my life where I felt let down, abandoned, or on the 'outside,' In my childhood, my family life revolved around three different families: my dad's, my mom's, and my stepmom's. It was challenging to feel truly connected to any of my extended family, as I struggled to find where I belonged. Then there was the story of my ex-fiancée and her family—they welcomed me with open arms, becoming an integral part of my life. Many holidays were spent with them. However, in May 2018, when the engagement fell apart at the last minute, so too did those family connections, leaving me feeling as though the support I had relied on, vanished suddenly. That on-off, cold turkey, letting go of support networks and building new ones, can be especially difficult when experienced during childhood. So, for those of you who know what I'm talking about, these instances of feeling "unsupported" can also be highly relevant.

Of course, now I'm with my wife, someone who supports me in countless ways. However, in this specific situation, I felt immensely let down and unsupported.

I struggled with; 'Why can't she have my back to finish off and complete this one thing that is so important to me?' 'Why can't she just be there for me?' These feelings of hurt and disappointment are projected as intense anger because I was emotionally overwhelmed, unable to identify or express the root cause of my anger.

As men, there's immense pressure to be providers and protectors. Sometimes, we long for relief from this role, even if momentarily. I see this often in my work with men—they want those rare moments when someone else takes the lead. That day, I felt overwhelmed and projected my fear of being let down onto my wife. Sometimes, we just long for our spouse or partner to step in and handle a task, giving us a break from the constant planning and responsibility. These instances of wanting support are rare for an independent person like me, but when they arise, they're crucial needs I long to be met.

Feeling unimportant, unsupported, or unappreciated often comes from unspoken expectations or past experiences. Communicating clearly about our fears and needs with our partners is crucial. We can't expect them to know our past or our expectations without sharing openly.

As human beings, we all have core needs: to feel seen, heard, loved, appreciated, and a sense of belonging. As men, beneath our anger often lies a feeling of being unseen, unheard, unappreciated, or unimportant. Addressing these needs with vulnerability and honest communication can be transformative in relationships.

Actionable Steps

1. **Recognizing Anger**
   - How do I usually respond to feelings of anger?
   - What are the thoughts that come into my head when I feel angry?
   - Do I try to justify my actions and place the blame for the anger on another person?
   - Can I identify healthy ways I can communicate my anger and feelings at that moment?

2. **Identifying Pressure Points**
   - What situations or circumstances lead me to feel pressured or stressed? Are they self-imposed or external?
   - How do I set expectations for myself and others? Are these expectations realistic?
   - How can I set boundaries and effectively communicate my limitations to reduce feelings of pressure?

3. **Perceptions of Wrongdoing**
   - What situations make me feel wronged or unfairly treated? Are these perceptions aligned with objective reality or influenced by insecurities and personal biases?
   - How do I typically respond when I feel wronged?
   - Are there patterns or recurring themes that I can identify to prevent similar situations in the future?

Understanding our Triggers

Do you have a trigger?

Chances are you have used this word or phrase to describe something that made you feel uncomfortable or elicited a reaction in you.

As we are becoming more aware of the importance of mental health in the mainstream media, words and phrases like "trigger", or "being triggered" have entered our everyday lives.

But what is a trigger? When should you use the word and how did it form?

In simple terms, triggers are knee-jerk reactions when our senses are overstimulated by recalling a traumatic event. It's important to note that this can happen on both a conscious and a subconscious level.

When we first have a traumatic experience, our brain stores sensory information with it, things like smells, sounds, and tastes. The common triggers are loud noises and yelling, certain holidays (Christmas, Easter), smells, or even being left alone.

Our brain is doing a 'wonderful job' by storing these triggers, to protect us and to prevent these situations from happening to us again in the future. But of course, it doesn't always get it right. It can also be deleterious when our trigger response kicks on when the situation doesn't warrant it, whether that is because it is not a dangerous situation, or because even if it is potentially dangerous, we are equipped with the tools, skills, and abilities to be able to handle such a situation safely.

My point here is not to go through every trigger that can exist, but to explain how you should approach triggers.

From my personal experience, there is a lot I can draw on about abandonment trauma and abandonment triggers. The underlying emotion is pretty clear, "Please don't leave me". But that is seldom what is being said or expressed. Nobody is going to come right out to you and say "Please physically stay next to me so I don't feel like you are running away.".

Instead, abandonment triggers manifest the other way. Most people with an abandonment wound will subconsciously or consciously push people away, the moments they start to realize they need them.

The mental program that we have installed sends a signal that says, "This person is going to leave me, and I will lose something".

To avoid this, the trigger will make the person push the other away because that act of pushing away hurts less than witnessing them leaving in the future.

This plays out in different ways for different triggers and situations.

As you start to recognize your triggers, your job will be to communicate what is happening to yourself and your partner.

Understand that there are multiple aspects of the way our triggers can play out. We have a surface level that gets expressed first, and then a hidden layer, or layers, that come next. This can feel very confusing.

This push-and-pull dynamic is characteristic of abandonment triggers and other triggers as well. I invite you to look and notice the discrepancies between thoughts, emotions, and actions and bring to light what is under the surface.

It takes a lot of time and a lot of patience to sit with yourself. Take time and conscious effort to measure your thoughts and your feelings. You may very well find that they won't match up in those situations. Plus, you will be left thinking, I am still sad, feeling abandoned, feeling lonely, whatever the case may be. Once you have a clearer understanding of your trigger(s), work to concretely lay out for yourself and your partner, how it manifests. Do so at both the surface and deeper levels. From there don't be afraid to take time to yourself when you're feeling triggered. Take time alone, even if it's for a couple of minutes so that you can gather your thoughts and emotionally regulate yourself. You can do this by doing some breathing exercises, splashing cold water on your face, or even doing 20 push-ups. Find what helps you come into balance and identify "Hey is what I'm feeling right now my trigger, or is this really how I'm feeling?" Sometimes it can be a little bit of both, but when our triggers are activated and we're not aware of it, it really distorts the way that we see things, and it definitely distorts our ability to be able to have healthy and effective communication around whatever it is that's bothering us.

Once you're regulated, have a conversation with your partner about where you are at and what you are working through. These conversations, emotional check-ins, and vulnerable shares will likely not feel smooth or come easy at first, but they will get better. They enhance our relationships and deepen our self-awareness.

Another big part of this is having an open conversation with our partner to say, "Hey, when you do this, it makes me feel this way."

Now, it's important to say that this is not done in an 'accusatory' way. Like; *"Well, when you do this, it makes me feel like this, so it's all your fault."*

No.

These are vulnerable, open, curious types of conversations.

For example;

"Hey, I noticed "x" the other day when you said "y". It started to make me feel "z" inside. Would you be willing to help me to unpack that? I'm

sure it wasn't your intention to make me feel this, but gosh, I was struggling with that afterward."

Do you see the stark contrast between those two statements? The more that we as men can have vulnerable and emotionally regulated conversations where we authentically show up and speak our heart and express our emotional wants and needs and set those healthy boundaries, the healthier the relationship will be with our wives and our partners.

Trust me guys, the women in our lives want us to be more open with them.

No partner is a mind reader, so our needs won't get met, unless we communicate in a clear and regulated way about what is working and not working for us and for the relationship.

Actionable Steps

1. **Identifying Triggers**
   - What experiences or situations evoke strong emotional or physical reactions?
   - How do they relate to specific traumatic events?
   - How does my brain respond to the trigger? What thoughts come up?
   - How does my body respond to the trigger? Where do I feel the sensation come up?

2. **Unspoken Emotions**
   - How do triggers reflect underlying, unexpressed emotions or fears? Can I verbalize these fears and thoughts to someone?
   - Do I recognize the confusion between my thoughts, emotions, and actions when triggered?
   - Can I organize them and discuss them with a professional?

3. **Relationship Building**

- How can I initiate conversations with my partner about my triggers without placing blame or accusations?
- Can I lead with openness and curiosity during those conversations?
- Do I understand that these discussions enhance the depth and quality of our relationship?

The Absence of War is Not Peace

The absence of war is not peace.

This is important to remember when thinking through conflict. Just because there is no war, it doesn't mean the generals are not preparing for battle.

Just because there is no war, it doesn't mean you have good relationships with your neighbors.

Just because there is no war, it doesn't mean there is a peace treaty.

When we bottle our thoughts, feelings, and emotions, it's like a battle stirring within us.

Initially, it manifests as anxiety. Left unaddressed, this suppressed anxiety can spiral into depression, anger, and further emotional turmoil.

In my work, particularly with men seeking counseling, I witness this struggle firsthand. I've grappled with it myself. They're puzzled, just as I was. Everything externally might seem fine—sure, there are daily stresses, but why this inexplicable anxiety? Where does this depression stem from?

The answer I keep coming back to time and time again is that it's internal. It brews from within us and from fears and insecurities we have not addressed. Just because there is no visible conflict in our surroundings doesn't mean there is inner peace. Our modern life guarantees chaos, this you must know. Even when we manage to gain control of our personal spaces and keep them calm, even if we have everything we might have wished for, unexpressed emotions fester like an undiscovered tumor and bring chaos.

It's a loop, you see? You first attempt to organize external chaos but neglect the core issues. Then, the internal turmoil that was always there escalates. Dysregulation leads to anger and explosions, and suddenly, we're back in chaos.

Very often in my work, I see men struggle to communicate their emotional wants and needs. There are many reasons for this. First, recent generations rarely have a male figure that models this behavior.

This leads to an even worse, twofold issue. One, a lack of guidance in expressing emotions, and two, a purposeful suppression. Adult male caretakers overtly or covertly encourage young boys to suppress their emotions. In other words, young boys are told to bury their feelings, leading to an internal tug of war later in life, which inevitably leads to internal chaos.

Boys are being set up to be at war with their adult self, mostly predicated upon years of suppressed emotions.

This suppression becomes even deeper if the father or male caretaker tells the boy to "toughen up" or "don't be a crybaby". In essence, it instills the belief that crying is a sign of weakness. We don't have to look far to see this male archetype in action. Western culture paints a picture of a hardened warrior that stands above "female" emotions. That, of course, makes the young boy feel that crying or expressing certain related emotions goes against societal expectations, family bonds, and interpersonal relationships.

I work with men who have been at an internal war with themselves for years, sometimes even decades. I see the damage that this causes to all aspects of their humanity. Again, this internal war goes back to their childhood, where learned behavior patterns directed them to suppress their feelings and emotions to maintain the status quo or give some illusion of peace.

By the time they reach the therapy chair, men have suppressed their thoughts and emotions for so long, that parts of them feel powerless. Unfortunately, this default mode is now ingrained in their subconscious programming.

The internal state: *Feelings of helplessness, powerlessness, unworthiness, and insecurity.*

The output: *Non-serving communication patterns that are ineffective (usually, anger-related).*

The result: *An environment that doesn't feel safe to their partner and continued unmet needs.*

So much frustration and resentment is built up, with no avenue other than verbal, and sadly, sometimes physical aggression. Altogether, a perfect recipe for the hyper-masculine to rear its ugly head and further hinder healthy emotional expression. The resentment and anger that are present are often directed towards their partner or back inwards at themselves.

Again, that angry outburst is a last-ditch effort to be seen and heard. Which will, nevertheless, still cause the man to continue to fail to get his needs met.

Lastly, as men act out in this aggressive way, women may feel unsafe and powerless. This is the cherry on top of an already damaged emotional basis. And here's the real kicker; even if these outbursts lead to moments where the woman acquiesces to the man's hypermasculine and angry outbursts, it's not truly coming from the heart and the relationship is weakened as the female companion is acting from a place of 'survivor mode.'

Actionable Steps

Now that we are moving further into the book, it is important to start thinking about new strategies, actions, and steps that you want to begin immediately. Here are a few suggestions. You can begin with the one that feels like the easiest option for you but I recommend trying a few before settling on one.

1. **Daily Journaling**
   - Set aside time each day to journal about feelings, triggers, and reactions to gain clarity and insights.

2. **Mindfulness Practice**
   - Find a set moment each day where you practice deep-breathing exercises and mindfulness. Before starting, think of a trigger that you want to work through. Calmly observe your thoughts and body during the process.

3. **Self-Care Routine**
   - Establish a simple, very quick self-care routine. Don't try to make it complicated or include too many things. You can involve activities like painting, exercise, or listening to music. Be intentional about using that time to work through stress and give yourself permission to find the flow.

The Power of Asking for Help

If you are thirsty and need water, but you don't tell your partner, can you blame them for not bringing you a glass?

A lot of the surface-level and sometimes deeper issues in relationships are similar to this.

We need something, we fail to ask for it, and then we jump on the blame train and expect our partner to understand.

One of the most important communication patterns is asking for and receiving help.

The reasons we fail to do so can be grouped into three main categories: hyper-independence, fear of rejection, and vulnerability concerns.

All of the above likely comes from past negative experiences in childhood, where a request for assistance or support was dismissed or criticized. The most harmful one is if we never felt safe to even ask for it to begin with.

If this was present in your childhood, the wounds and trauma run deep.

A lot of women fall into these categories. They don't want to be perceived as a burden and place their needs in the insignificant or trivial category.

As a result, the man in this situation never gets the chance to rise to the occasion and support them.

The same can also be said about the men. But they do express it a bit differently. Instead of shifting the blame onto themselves and saying "I don't want to bother you." they might instead say, "You don't look after me."

If this back-and-forth style of communication is something you relate to, then chances are you have been exposed to repeated rejection trauma when previously expressing your needs. It is possible to resolve it, but will likely require you to dig very deep to do so.

In my counseling experience, I've rarely encountered a woman in a reasonably healthy relationship refusing to meet her husband's expressed needs. Their missteps are more likely to be parentification, shifting the blame onto themselves, or shutting down emotionally. To refuse it outright rarely happens. These differences are not expressed to vilify one sex and praise the other. Both situations are wrong. Both situations prohibit healthy expression and communication.

When we begin to assign significance to the degree of blame, we miss the whole picture. If your relationship is a meal, then the recipe is the ingredients you bring into the relationship.

But something strange happens and we forget, we love this meal. We can't wait to have this food, and we've worked hard to prepare it. This is our favorite meal ever, and one we want to enjoy every day. Then why is it when we bring ill-advised ingredients to the kitchen and then get annoyed when it doesn't taste good anymore? It's important to ask our partner what they want and need and to clearly tell them what we want and need.

Guys, it's crucial to consider how your needs might be *implied* but not *explicitly communicated.*

Which then leads us to having a conversation about the words that we use when communicating with our wives and partners about this idea of needs. You see, our words, and the way we express them, hold immense weight in shaping our realities, whether for better or worse.

Ryan Joseph Kopyar

A few months ago, before a trip to Whistler, British Columbia, my wife and I had one of those disagreements that was pretty serious. The next day during breakfast, we delved into the impact of specific words during the disagreement, specifically focusing on "disappointment."

For me, "disappointment" is a relatively light word. If I were to miss out on an ice cream sundae because they were out of ice cream, I might casually say, "Ah, I'm disappointed." My wife has a different reaction to the word.

It triggers a sense of failing at being a good spouse or accomplishing certain tasks. That feeling of 'not measuring up' makes her hesitant to continue trying as if failure once means why bother trying again? So, for her, the word "disappointment" holds a much deeper impact. This realization unfolded as we discussed various things the next day, in a more relaxed environment after the heated disagreement. Which by the way, is the best time to have those discussions and be able to resolve them.

In recognizing how much weight this word carries for my wife, we agreed that 'disappointment' is a feeling everyone experiences, and it's okay to feel disappointed. She said she will work on her internal healing as it relates to the feelings this word triggers. On the other hand, I thought of other words I use that I need to be aware of.

I realized that I used the word "unacceptable," a lot, even though it was not a feeling that I was trying to express at that moment. While expressing disappointment as a feeling is acceptable, conveying something as "unacceptable" needed adjustment in my language. To this day, I can still say the word disappointed, because expressing our feelings to each other is healthy. At the same time, I make sure to be clear that I am disappointed in the situation and not her specifically.

As you start to unpack your own trigger words and learn how to express your feelings, know that you will make mistakes.

• • •

Big Boys Do Cry

I want to encourage you to have open conversations with your spouse or your partner. Talk about the words that you use. Ask each other; "How can I best support you?" or "What is it that you need from me at this moment?" Trust me guys, so very often the main thing that the woman in our life is looking for is someone to hold space for them. And when we hold space for them, that opens up the door for them to want to meet our emotional wants and needs. Everyone's 'love language' is different. 'Help' can look different based on the person and even the context of the situation. Either way, effective help is never going to be delivered or received, without an open, emotionally regulated dialogue around it.

Not only that, but you are going to disappoint people, your partner included. That doesn't mean that you have 'failed' the person or you are stuck in a permanent state of failure. It means that in that particular situation, it didn't work out the way you had hoped for.

Disagreements, disappointments, and setbacks can take on a different meaning depending on how you choose to look at them.

Finding out your favorite restaurant is closed, might mean you stumble across your new favorite, with much better food. Disappointing your partner with your choice of words or actions is not the end of the relationship. It may finally allow you to have a deep conversation about unmet needs and come out stronger because of it.

Actionable Steps

If you haven't started practicing the suggestions of previous chapters, this is the time to do so. We will start easy.

1. **Create a "safe" word**
   - Establish a neutral word or signal with your partner that indicates when one of you feels triggered or uncomfortable. Allow for a set amount of time or a pause before further discussion.

2. **Try a role reversal exercise**
   - Switch roles with your partner and take turns expressing needs. Try to verbalize things they have told you they need or the emotional needs they have expressed in the past.

3. **Practice real-world, "ask for help" challenges**
   - Sign up for a workshop or activity with your partner where you need to collaborate and ask for help from others to succeed.
   - Find small real-life situations where you practice asking for small tasks or help from people in your life. Gradually progress to incorporating personal needs and emotional support.

Improving Communication

You know by now that communication stands as the cornerstone of a thriving relationship. When disputes escalate individuals feel disregarded or misunderstood, leading to blame rather than nurturing healthy dialogue. It can feel like someone is attacking you, literally. But of course that is not what is happening. It is a cycle that can easily become toxic and that brings nothing of value to either party.

I get called to help people improve their communication both in one-on-one sessions and during couples counseling a lot.

During those couples sessions, it's like one person is saying, "I'm communicating so clearly," while the other is hearing something completely different!

Helping couples bridge that gap is what I'm all about.

Here's the scoop: Men and women often chat from different mental arenas. Women are cruising through convo-land on the emotional highway, using the right side of the brain. Meanwhile, guys are cruising in the logic lane on the left side.

But hey, this isn't about one being 'right or wrong'. It's more about this communication disconnect that happens. What I want you to remember is that there is space in the middle where you can meet.

For women, it's about finding more zen and reigning in those emotions a bit. At the same time, men need to move away from overthinking and get into the 'heart groove' of the matter.

Without being too critical, I find women can tap into logic a lot easier than men can tap into their emotions. After all, this is the reason why I am writing this book in the first place. The key to navigating those conversations and improving your communication can be as clear as tapping into your heart space and allowing connection.

It's like speaking your partner's language by pouring some heart and emotions into the conversation. The first thing you will notice is that you stop talking past each other, and can meet on the same wavelength.

But keep in mind, that shift shouldn't happen because you "must do it". It isn't about scoring extra points from your spouse or finding inner peace so she doesn't nag you. It is a practice that will benefit all other relationships in your life as well.

The goal is to replace this cycle with mutual understanding and support, to nourish the relationship.

Here are some scenarios and language to keep in mind while trying to improve your communication.

1. **Empathy and Vulnerability:** Healthy communication stands on a ground of empathy, vulnerability, and the willingness to set aside personal ego and pride. With these ingredients, you can achieve impartial communication and resolve conflicts.
2. **Setting the tone:** Healthy communication means addressing concerns without assigning blame. For instance, when feeling undervalued, expressing emotions without pointing fingers and accusing:
3. **Intentional Phrasing:** Using phrases like "I'm sure it wasn't your intention" softens the conversation, highlighting that the goal is not to harm but to express feelings.

Husband: "I feel unappreciated when my efforts go unnoticed. I appreciate your feedback but acknowledging my actions would mean a lot to me."

Wife: "When you came home and only said the place looks good, it made me feel unappreciated. Acknowledging specific aspects of the decoration would make me feel seen and appreciated."

Empathetic Responses and Collaborative Solutions:

1. **Acknowledging Feelings:** Responding with empathy reinforces appreciation for the partner's vulnerability:

Wife: "I appreciate your vulnerability. It wasn't my intention to make you feel unappreciated.

Husband: "I didn't mean to make you feel unseen. Your effort in decorating is valued."

2. **Collaborative Problem-Solving:** Proposing solutions and inviting feedback signifies a commitment to the relationship:

Wife: "Moving forward what are your thoughts on how I can best make you feel appreciated? Let's discuss adjustments together."

Husband: "I appreciate you so much. How can I best show this appreciation next time?"

The Childhood Effect

The other day, I witnessed a powerful moment with my wife's daughter. As she walked up the stairs, she began pounding her feet, announcing, "I'm very angry right now." I asked her if she wanted a hug, and she said 'NO!'. I chuckled and took a step back. Here is a young person who has already learned to vocalize her wants and needs. I was proud of her for refusing help she didn't want. It also sparked a reflection on the profound impact of childhood communication lessons.

Women and men go through this stage a bit differently.

For little girls, these are the moments where their boundaries are tested and often eroded. They say they don't want to hug their uncle, but then they are forced to kiss on the cheek. On the other hand, little boys might face a different kind of communication lesson. They might be taught not to cry or show emotions openly, as it's sometimes associated with 'not what little boys do.' They might hear phrases like "big boys don't cry" or be discouraged from expressing vulnerability or sensitivity. This early conditioning might lead them to suppress emotions, which can affect their communication and emotional expression in relationships later in life.

Growing up, there were times I didn't feel encouraged to voice my thoughts, feelings, or emotions. Perhaps not that I felt unsafe, but rather that I wasn't allowed to freely express myself in certain situations.

This upbringing significantly influences our communication patterns in adulthood. If we were taught to suppress emotions, we might bottle them up as adults. This internalization deeply affects relationships. When we're conditioned not to express certain emotions, we tend to stifle them within ourselves.

For men, this mostly comes through as a reluctance to say they need help. They feel as though it is NOT OK to say they are overwhelmed and are unsure how to cope.

As we've spoken about, internalizing thoughts and emotions isn't healthy. It's like a ticking time bomb within us. So, here's a challenge: reflect on emotions you might have been discouraged from acknowledging as a child. What were those feelings that you couldn't openly share because it didn't seem safe or acceptable to do so?

Consider how these childhood experiences might unknowingly influence your present relationships. There's a possibility that without consciously realizing it, you might withhold, refrain from sharing, or struggle to be vulnerable about those particular emotions. These patterns often stem from experiences where expressing certain feelings led to repercussions or judgments.

A therapist or counselor can help you create a safe place to travel back to that time. Imagine being seven, feeling a certain way, and being reprimanded for it. These incidents, repeated over time, could have taught us to keep such emotions hidden to avoid punishment. The impact? Carrying these suppressed emotions into our relationships, sometimes without even recognizing it.

These unexpressed feelings, harbored for so long, can have a major impact on our current relationships. It's a profound realization to understand how our past experiences with what was safe to communicate and what wasn't, can influence our present ability or willingness to express and share emotions within our relationships.

Actionable Steps

These exercises are meant to be done with your partner or loved one. Make sure to pick a suitable time when both of you are open to hearing and can take the time to be present emotionally and physically.

1. **Childhood reflection activity**

   - Set aside dedicated time with your partner to discuss childhood experiences related to communication.
   - Structure the conversation by sharing specific instances where emotions were discouraged or suppressed. For example, recall an event where expressing certain emotions led to repercussions or judgment. Discuss the impact of these experiences on present communication patterns. Encourage empathetic listening and a non-judgmental environment to foster understanding.

2. **Shared journaling exercise**

   - Start an emotional expression journal with your partner. Dedicate a specific time each week to write about suppressed emotions of the last week or feelings that you didn't bring up.

- Reflect on why or what was happening in your head and you chose not to bring them up.
- Include any triggers from your childhood or past experiences.

3. **Role reversal exercise**

- Designate an evening to role-play conversations that you see as standard in your relationship
- Each partner should embody the other's typical communication style and responses.
- Take turns trying to understand and empathize with the other's perspective.

Navigating Conflict

Let's dive into the realm of conflict, a space brimming with intricacies and challenges.

There is no relationship without conflict.

However, when we withhold parts of ourselves, hide our emotions, and suppress our feelings, conflict becomes all the more challenging.

The goal is not to be without conflict but to practice strategies that allow conflict to be resolved and to grow more connected as a result. In relationships where one or both individuals act with fear, secrecy, and concealment, conflict is overwhelming.

This is the type of conflict that runs unchecked, becomes intimidating, and divisive. We are briefly going to discuss how conflict should look when the aim is to build nurturing healthy connections.

Within conflicts, the term "anger" frequently takes center stage. We have already discussed anger in previous chapters so this is a good time to revisit that. It's crucial to distinguish between "I'm angry" and "I'm angry with you." Let that sink in for a moment. The difference between these two statements holds significant weight in relationships.

Challenge yourself to delve deeper beyond the surface level. Ask yourself, "Am I genuinely angry with my wife, girlfriend, or partner? Or is my anger directed toward something or someone else entirely?" Often, our emotions manifest as "I'm angry with you," but there's a transformative shift when we rephrase it as "I'm angry about this situation."

● ● ●

94

Expressing this distinction—saying "I'm angry, and I love you" or "I'm feeling lonely right now, and I love you"—is a game-changer. That inclusion of "I love you" is key to maintaining connection. While we're discussing anger, this principle applies to any range of emotions.

I get it guys, I know that adding in this part of "...and I love you" - it is not 'natural' for us. We weren't taught this, and it's very unlikely that we saw the men in our lives demonstrating this. But this is part of the secret sauce here, this is what I'm talking about when I encourage making the shift from the left brain into the right brain. Adding 'I love you' at the end acts as the key that unlocks the door for your wife or your partner to hear and receive the totality of what you said.

You can be angry at a person, or you can be frustrated by circumstances, an event, or an experience. The two are hard to distinguish when you are sitting too close to the problem. As you go on this journey, it is important to distinguish between the moments where you felt anger toward your partner versus the moments where you directed anger at them.

Another big key to navigating conflict is practicing active listening.

This isn't just about *hearing* the words, it is about *understanding* the emotions, concerns, and needs behind the words. It also involves creating a safe space for your partner to express themselves without judgment or interruption.

Let me be clear, active listening is not about being criticized, belittled, or abused. It is about valuing the person you have opposite you, so you can provide them with a space that will allow them to express themselves.

Think back to the times you felt unheard or misunderstood.

I am willing to bet you said something along the lines of, "Just let me finish!" or "Give me a second to express my thoughts."

It is truly a challenge to stop yourself in those moments and provide that space to the other one. This is because resolving conflict can feel like 'winning or losing'. This creates a destructive power play, where one or both people attempt to overpower the other with logic, emotions, and facts.

This is also why men often have two approaches: say nothing or explode in anger.

There is a core memory I want to share that relates to this and is not focused on a partnership dynamic, but a family one.

My father, sitting at the kitchen table overwhelmed in the middle of an argument, head in his hands. My stepmother and I were disagreeing. My dad was faced with conflict but didn't have the tools to navigate what he wanted to communicate. Was I to guess, I would say his issue was seeing his partner and his son fighting over something trivial and feeling lost. At that moment, he had many options, but he chose to say and do nothing. I often wonder how differently it could've played out if my dad had the tools to navigate his emotions, communicate them better and help navigate the emotions of the disagreement between my step-mother and I. Perhaps you're in a similar situation, grappling with family chaos, feeling lost within your own emotions. Maybe you need help identifying and expressing those emotions.

With that in context, let's get back to the two common approaches of *saying nothing* or *exploding in anger*. When we play the game with these two options, we will lose every time, even if there are moments where it feels like we 'won.'

Because you will have lost the safety net, the trust, and the empathy that the other person is requesting.

Healthy conflict resolution involves compromise and a mutual willingness to understand each other's perspectives. The commitment to finding solutions needs to come from both sides, to benefit the relationship.

So, I will ask you again. Are you ready to let go of your ego and old triggers and instead bring self-awareness, vulnerability, active listening, and commitment to growth? Are you ready to stop focusing on 'winning' and start focusing on connection and healing?

Emotional Flexibility

You heard about active listening, now it is time to discuss emotional flexibility.

This is not about mental gymnastics and rationalizations, no.

Emotional flexibility is a transformative stage of self-awareness.

Without self-awareness, we can rarely, if ever, achieve sustainable growth. The reason I bring up emotional flexibility now is because I hope you have at this stage, realized and are ready to take responsibility for your part in these situations.

To understand emotional flexibility is about distinguishing between what we feel and who we are. You might be wondering, but surely, my emotions are part of what I am, correct? Well, no!

We are not what we feel, but we do become what we believe.

Our emotions and feelings can be used as a guide to the right answer, but they are not always forthcoming with the information they provide on the surface level. We feel our emotions, but that doesn't mean that what we feel is objective truth.

Picture this: "I feel angry" versus "I am angry". There is a vast chasm between the two as we already discussed. Even though you feel angry, that doesn't make you "angry".

The skill of emotional flexibility starts with the premise of this realization. You need to be able to say that you have these thoughts, feelings, and emotions, but you are NOT your thoughts, feelings, and emotions.

The second arena where emotional flexibility plays a huge role is apologizing.

That doesn't only mean saying "I'm sorry", but knowing when to apologize, how, and why. Apologizing or admitting mistakes often involves discomfort.

When you have been carrying anger, resentment, fears, and traumas, being asked to apologize feels like an extra uncomfortable burden that is simply too much. For men who strive for perfection, this becomes even more complex.

You were possibly raised to believe that perfection is the standard and that your role as a primary provider should be enough. As you practice being that provider, you are rewarded with compliments, respect, and admiration. The moment a complaint arises, however, it feels like all your hard work is being dismissed.

Emotional flexibility is what needs to enter your toolbox to approach admitting imperfections as a good thing. It's not weakness that will make you say "sorry" but empowerment. You are so secure, confident, and appreciated within your role, that acknowledging one, two, or even three errors will be inconsequential.

Your role at that moment is to embrace feedback to avoid repeating those mistakes. You are allowed to make mistakes, as you are allowed to admit those mistakes and do better next time.

As we have discussed, this particular dynamic of 'perfection' often stems from childhood.

Most of the men that I work with weren't allowed to make mistakes as little kids. Not only that, but they attached their worth to a type of performance that brought accolades. As a little kid, you separated your worth into things that could be measured to receive the love you needed. Maybe that recognition brought rewards that felt like an acknowledgment; a bicycle as a gift, a phone, 'curfew privileges', or even a much-needed word of encouragement from a caregiver.

In situations like these, we are made to feel that our worthiness of receiving love is solely predicated and tied to our ability to perform whatever role it is that we are in at that time. For instance, if I'm a student, I need to be earning A's to be deserving of love. If I am a hockey player, I need to score goals, to be deserving of love. And so, you see how as adult men, in the role of provider, there is no room for error, our mental program makes us feel as though we need to be perfect to be loved.

Wow, guys!

Is that fair to do to ourselves?

Don't we deserve to be more flexible with ourselves?!

These are all incredibly complex dynamics that can require unpackaging in a safe space, with a trained professional.

Emotional flexibility marks a transformative stage in self-awareness. It's about distinguishing between what we feel and who we are. Another example we could use is; "I feel I can't do enough" versus "I am not enough."

Very different!

Understanding this disparity forms the bedrock of emotional flexibility.

As primary providers, men often face immense pressure to excel financially. But this pressure isn't confined to just work; it's a mental exercise that must change. It's okay to falter, to say sorry, to acknowledge errors. By doing so, we step away from our need to control that stems from fear.

You can even consider this act of apologizing as an invitation to your partner to participate in your healing journey. Can you embrace having the courage to say, "I'm still learning. Can you help me?"

I've experienced this firsthand in my marriage and will speak about it later in this book. The moments I acknowledged my shortcomings and invited my wife to support me in those areas, transformed my marriage.

The crux of emotional flexibility isn't about being perfect but about being open to growth.

Actionable Steps

These exercises aim to foster mutual understanding of past emotional wounds and create a better framework for resolving future conflict.

1. **Reflection first**

   - Set aside time individually to reflect on moments from the past when negative comments or hurtful words were directed at you.
   - Journal about these instances, detailing the specific words or phrases used, the context in which they were said, and how they made you feel at that time.
   - Encourage your partner to do the same, reflecting on any negative comments or hurtful words they've experienced in the past.

2. **Shared discussion**

   - Choose a specific time to sit together and share your reflections. Create a safe and supportive environment for this discussion, ensuring both of you feel comfortable and respected.
   - Take turns sharing your experiences with negative comments. Use phrases like "I recall when...." or "It hurt me when..." to express the impact of those words on your emotions.
   - Listen actively to your partner's experiences without interrupting or judging. Validate their feelings and acknowledge the significance of their emotions linked to those words.

3. Acknowledgment and empathy

- After sharing, take a moment to acknowledge the hurt caused by those negative comments. Express empathy towards each other's past experiences, recognizing the pain those words might have inflicted.
- Avoid placing blame or trying to rationalize the words spoken. Instead, focus on validating the emotions felt during those instances.

Holding it in

As we have discussed, one of the biggest things that I work on with men is the notion of holding it in. Men often hold their thoughts, feelings, and emotions inside for too long. So long that it becomes unsustainable. Then the inevitable happens. The bubble pops and the emotional outburst (whether emotional or physical) occurs. We previously touched on this in the chapter on "The Absence of War is Not Peace".

This chapter will focus more on how to express your emotional needs and how to spot the roadblocks that exist along the way. Before we dive deeper into the why, and how to prevent that, it is important to emphasize what I mentioned earlier.

Bottling it all in doesn't define strength. Holding it all in doesn't make you tough. I know that's what we've been told most of our lives, but it simply is not true! Life is so incredibly tough. And it's safe to say, without even knowing you, that you have faced your share of hardships.

Holding the pain inside is not what makes you tough. I did it. It did it for a long three decades. I held the pain from the death of my mother and unborn sister, as well as a host of other things. It was too long and it didn't help.

The one thing I can promise you is that life gets better once we connect and begin to release our pain. It starts slow, but it soon becomes more and more liberating.

How do we get started?

I'm going to teach you some of those ways. It's an ongoing process and I'm still executing it myself. But it is possible.

Expressing Emotional Needs

Many men I work with grapple with feeling unworthy of sharing their emotional needs. The catch is this. Even when these needs get buried deep down, they still resurface, but not in a healthy way.

The role of a counselor is to be a healthy outlet for these emotions with no judgment or fear.

So men will come to me and let me into the deepest aspects of their humanity; their thoughts, emotions, feelings, wants, and needs. The common threads are that these men have unexpressed and unfulfilled wants and needs, which leaves them feeling empty inside.

When I ask them if they've shared these wants and needs with their wife or spouse, they say no.

In my experience working with couples, this becomes a root cause for issues down the road. You see, buried needs tend to erupt in anger or aggression, they rarely come out in a healthy way, and they feel like an attack.

And what happens in that situation? Well, the need doesn't get met. We feel like we said it and expressed it, but it wasn't in a healthy way. And then what happens? Well, it goes unmet. And so we say, "See, I told my wife what I needed, and she didn't provide it to me."

This is where the cycle then begins. More frustration, and more suppressing of emotional wants and needs. Then isolation. You might start thinking that if you bury it, it will pass, but it won't.

Your wife or partner is waiting for you to express it. Not only that, but they would love for you to do so. They are looking for that emotional connection and crave it. So what do you do?

I encourage discussing these needs when things are going well, really well. The reason is that when things are going well, our guards are down. We are more receptive and open to giving and receiving feedback. You might be thinking, "Oh, but things are going so well, why would I cause an issue." To that, I say, "I hear you, but this is the ideal environment or conditions for having these types of conversations."

That is precisely the best time to bring it up. You can start by saying to your partner that you love them and it is so great to be sharing this moment with them. Then you open a discussion about how you feel when she meets your needs, and what unmet wants or needs you have. You share your thoughts, your feelings, and your perspective. There is no judgment, no shame, no fear. This is how I feel.

When you start the conversation this way, you open the room for honest discussion.

For example, "Hey honey, I never told you, but when you kiss me good morning before work it means the world to me. Thank you. Can you please do it more often?"

I can't tell you how much you will be blown away when you start to express your needs on that level, with a positive and loving tone.

Your partner is waiting for it. You want to say it. (Don't lie to me man, I know you do!) Both will walk away feeling validated and loved. You will have expressed your wants and needs and your partner will feel safe and aware to provide more of it.

The act of opening up allows your partner the opportunity to meet those needs. Without that discussion, how would they know? You are essentially robbing them of the chance to do good things for you.

Don't be fooled into thinking you should be able to read your partner's mind. Nobody knows what the other wants until they express it. No matter how long you've been with this person.

When we appreciate that we are unique human beings, and complex ones as well, we realize we have a responsibility to speak up. When you get specific with what you need, what makes you feel good, and what your love language is, you are setting you and your partner up for success.

Stop Playing Defense

When we hide, withhold, and refrain from expressing feelings, we are essentially playing defense.

Our bodies and our brains prepare for a negative outcome and as a result, we are less likely to listen to what the other person has to say. When we enter a defensive state, it's akin to raising mental and emotional barriers. It's not about physical defenses but rather an internal guarding mechanism. In essence, our ego feels threatened.

We all possess egos, and when they're triggered, this emotional wall rises almost instinctively, aiming to shield us from potential harm or hurt. Subconsciously, this defensive wall emerges due to past experiences of being hurt or let down. It's like an automatic response, signaling that it's not safe to communicate openly.

Picture this: in a disagreement with a partner, I might deeply yearn for connection and understanding, yet my defensive emotional or mental stance blocks this expression. It's like having our defenses up while trying to reveal what our heart truly seeks; these two states can't coexist. This defensive mode hampers our chance of attaining what we genuinely desire at that moment.

Consequently, this blocks the possibility of genuine connection, leaving us feeling angry, sad, more isolated, and less understood. Learning to navigate through this isn't easy; it's an advanced skill in managing vulnerability within relationships. It's a process that takes time and conscious awareness. Even as someone trained in this field, I continue to work on it myself. The good news is that as you work on it, you are more aware of when you do it.

Big Boys Do Cry

Recognizing our defensive mode during disagreements or conflicts is crucial. It's about understanding that in that defensive state, we're forfeiting our chances to fulfill our genuine emotional needs.

I invite you to work towards training your brain to understand that taking the road of holding things inside will not lead to the outcome you want in your heart. It is like saying, here is an easy, grassy, flat path that leads endlessly into the woods. Then there is an uphill, rocky, and frankly quite scary path that leads to a spring. You want and need water, so you must take the second road. But you keep thinking that the flat road will be the one that takes you to the spring, when in reality it never will.

Actionable Steps

These exercises aim to cultivate a safe environment for open dialogue about emotional needs and encourage partners to express themselves vulnerably.

1. **Open Dialogue**

   - First, take some time independently to reflect on moments where you didn't express what you needed in the relationship.
   - Schedule a quiet time and make sure you are entering with a positive and judgment-free mind.
   - Start by expressing gratitude and love for your partner.
   - Share specific instances where your partner positively impacted your emotions.
   - Use phrases like, "I feel loved and connected when…" or "It means a lot to me when...".
   - Commit to open communication and conversations during the week/month or at a time when it makes sense to you both.

Getting Out of Your Head and Into Your Heart

Men lean heavily towards logical, left-brain thinking. This is shaped by our culture, and upbringing but also supported by various studies on human brain structure.

In our society, men are expected to be problem solvers and pragmatic thinkers. While this mindset serves well in many situations, it can create a disconnect in emotional connections, especially within relationships. My observations, based on personal experiences, interactions with friends, and my professional practice, support this.

Let's start with the positives. There are many positive aspects to this left-brain dominance. It provides men with confidence and the ability to quickly access, assess, and solve problems in their personal and professional lives and is an overall, good quality to have.

Then why do we often speak about it as though it is bad?

Because it should be a supporting quality and not the full package.

The external factor that contributes the most to staying stuck in this left-brain mode is societal expectations. In our Western culture, men are often discouraged from engaging with or connecting to the more creative and emotional aspects associated with women and the Divine Feminine energy.

Big Boys Do Cry

On the other hand, we encourage men to be less emotional and expressive. This is a time bomb when it comes to intimate conversations and genuine connection.

When men remain heavily rooted in their logical and pragmatic left brain, a disconnection in relationships is bound to occur.

I want to be clear. The goal here isn't to dismiss logic but to create space for emotional connection.

I am not saying, logic = bad, emotions = good. Not at all. If anything, leading just with emotions can be equally if not as detrimental.

The reason I am making this caveat is because I can hear the excuses that start to play in your brain.

No, I am not saying you need to be a drama queen or start crying in front of everyone all the time. I am not suggesting that logic is bad or that you need to change and become more "woman-like".

What I am saying is that you have within you the capacity for both. One has been suppressed and is underutilized. Your thoughts, emotions, wants, and needs were always there. You are not asked to create them. It's likely that you were taught to express them less, or not at all. It is also likely you were taught to express them in a manner that doesn't serve your emotional needs.

As a logical-oriented person, I invite you to realize that effective communication is not just about thoughts. It is about understanding and speaking from a shared emotional space.

Before we delve deeper into how we will do that, let's discuss the why.

Why is that shared emotional space so hard to occupy for men?

One of the answers is trauma!

Trauma

Unfortunately, almost every single one of us will experience trauma in our lives. Yet, we are not all affected by trauma in the same way.

Different events, different people, and different ages, all influence how trauma will affect us.

This chapter on trauma should come with a trigger warning.

I can't sugarcoat trauma. My role is to present a mirror and ask you to walk up to it and face the person staring back at you.

Either way, trauma is unpleasant.

Most men I work with have experienced it.

What is interesting is that some will come right out and say what happened and how it affects them to this day from the first session. Others will hint at it but seem almost unaware of the effects that this trauma has had or is having on them. Others will mention it at some point but later revert to hiding it.

Human emotions are complex, and when you add trauma it can be even more complex. The reason I know this is simple. I've experienced and faced my traumas, particularly the loss of my mother and unborn sister.

If you experienced trauma at a young age, it might be even worse. It is scientifically proven that individuals who have experienced trauma earlier on in life are significantly more susceptible to develop PTSD later on in life if re-exposed to additional traumatic experiences.

The other thing these individuals tend to struggle with is organizing their emotions. This also means they struggle to identify what their emotions are and how to express them.

Why would that be important, you ask?

Because being able to self-regulate and navigate your emotions is the first step to communicating and practicing vulnerability. Without that emotional connection, you are likely going through life feeling unfulfilled, unattached, unappreciated, and lost. As we store trauma, we store feelings, thoughts, and actions that accompany it.

I like to think of trauma as a non-serving energy that has been stored up in your body. Imagine this as a fire that is burning inside your body. You may or may not have a conscious awareness that this fire is burning inside your body. The longer the fire burns, the more potential there is for it to have a deleterious impact on you, and the more potential there is for that fire to spread to different people and situations around you.

This storing of trauma can go something like this.

We have a traumatic event. Within that event, there's an energetic experience. That energy gets stored inside our body. And unless we release it, we've got this little bit (or maybe BIG BIT) of chaos sitting underneath the surface.

Then, a trigger!

Our partner says something or does something that disrupts our emotional balance. Suddenly, we find ourselves dysregulated, upset, socially isolated, and increasingly unable to soothe or regulate our thoughts.

All of these are normal responses to a trauma trigger. They can also lead to incredibly unhealthy coping mechanisms. When this chaos is released towards our loved ones (partner, wife, family unit) the damage can be intense. They have no clue why we behave this way, and to be fair, we don't either. They try to help but are met with our defense mechanisms of avoidance, anger, resentment, and isolation. They try to love on us to bring down the guards. We may not only succeed in defending our guarded walls, but we might even bring out some of the emotional weapons to the defensive counter-attack.

I've heard so many partners say to their men, "Hey, I want to help." The same way I've heard so many men say, "I don't know how to accept their help, I want to but I can't."

These encounters—where partners express their willingness to assist and men yearn for change but feel locked within their turmoil—create a tug-of-war within relationships. It's like navigating a labyrinth without a map. Both partners are frustrated and disconnected.

For men harboring unresolved traumas, these interactions often lead to a deeper internal conflict. They want to express, connect, and reciprocate their partner's earnestness, but the invisible chains of unresolved trauma constrict their emotional freedom. It's a heart-wrenching struggle—knowing what to do but feeling bound by unseen forces.

Imagine being on the verge of healing. You have a partner that loves and respects you. You have a life you've worked hard for. Then, skeletons from the closet start to come up. You are ready to step through the door, but the weight of past wounds is holding you back.

This is an emotional paradox that is all too common.

If you have experienced it, know that you are not alone.

The desire for change intertwines with the fear of the unknown.

Breaking free from these chains is daunting, especially when they're rooted in trauma. It's like trying to dismantle a wall with one push, even though you've been building it for a lifetime. The good news is that healing is possible, and the path to healing starts with this acknowledgment of how your trauma is impacting you.

Acknowledgment will not erase the past, but it's the catalyst for change. It's the first beam of light in the dark tunnel of emotional healing. It's acknowledging that the trauma exists, that it impacts us, and that it's okay to seek help.

Big Boys Do Cry

As we have talked before, this isn't about rewriting history. What happened, has already happened. This is about reclaiming the meaning we assign to it for our present and future. By changing the meaning we give to our past, we alter the emotional charge that we have associated with it. Trauma is stored non-serving energy, and by shifting the meaning that we give to the trauma, we begin to shift, change and transmute the emotional charge that has been stored with it.

This two-part process of both releasing the non-serving energy as well as redefining the meaning of the event is crucial. So now in the present day when we recall the event, it has a more serving energy to it. An energy that helps to propel us forward.

For instance, for so long I had a negative energy associated with the tragic death of my mother and unborn sister. After my healing, I decided to give a meaning to that event within the following context, "I have experienced pain in my life, and it was an invitation for me to connect more to my heart. I am now going to use what I learned in this process to help others navigate their pain."

You see, I have not changed the event, but I have changed the associated meaning of the event.

As you think about all we have talked about so far, picture a life where you can engage with your emotions. A life where vulnerability isn't seen as a weakness but as an act of courage. Picture conversations where your trauma triggers no longer limit you, and you can express yourself without fear of judgment or rejection. This isn't an elusive dream; it's a tangible reality waiting on the other side of healing.

The lingering effects of trauma are an invitation, a beckoning toward a journey of self-discovery. As you move forward on your healing journey, you will realize that the effects of the trauma are not written in stone, but in a malleable storyline, an energetic experience that you can reshape in a way that serves you. This way helps you connect with individuals, especially those that you love, on a deep and meaningful level. Your trauma can be a chapter in your life that doesn't define you in a negative way, but one that has shaped your resilience and capacity for healing.

Actionable Steps

Trauma is never easy to talk about. You are not a therapist to your partner, remember that! But you can create space to acknowledge and address how those traumas come into the relationship.

1. **Self-reflect**

   - Write down moments or experiences from your past that might have caused emotional distress, turmoil, or discomfort.
   - When was the last time you felt triggered by something that happened in the past?

2. **Create a healing plan**

   - You can only go so far on your own.
   - Discuss the idea of seeking therapy or counseling with your loved one, either individually or together, to work through unresolved traumas.

3. **Rewrite the narrative**

   - Consider how you can reframe the experiences of past trauma into moments that contributed to growth and resilience.
   - Rather than focusing on how they defined your past, focus on how you will shape them to help your future.

4. **Continue the growth journey**

   - There are so many great books, documentaries, YouTube videos, and speeches on healing from trauma. Start by following some creators or buying a new book to read during the week.

That Broken Little Boy Inside

Do you see yourself as a boy or as a man?

If I were to ask you this question at work or around friends, you probably would say the latter.

But what about other areas of your life? What about the way you approach your feelings or the way you communicate with your partner? It doesn't matter if you are strong, capable, successful, or even have quite a few trips around the sun during your time here on earth.

Here's what I have come to realize, guys:

Inside every angry, frustrated, depressed, anxious man is a broken little boy.

In present day moments of dysregulation, that broken little boy *wants*, no, he feels he **NEEDS** to come out and make a fuss.

But what is really happening is that little boy is *calling for help and attention*. He's waiving a **red flag** saying, "hold up, something's wrong here!"

You might think of this as an oversimplification but it is true.

Dick Schwartz, who is the founder and creator of Internal Family Systems Therapy (IFS), speaks in length about this when he explores the different parts that make up the "self". Without getting overly clinical, IFS operates from the premise that we all have different parts within us. Think of it as multiple parts, or versions of ourselves. (This is in a healthy way and not a pathological one like multiple personality disorder.)

The different parts of ourselves run with their own agenda, mission, and goals. Ultimately, however, these different parts of us are all trying to keep us safe. These parts also have different fears and can respond in ways that confuse us. This is why it is so common to hear someone say, "Part of me is confused or doesn't want to do this."

While it is not the purpose of this book to delve into Internal Family Systems Therapy, it is important to understand how these parts developed, specifically the parts that were exposed to trauma.

When parts are exposed to trauma, they develop coping mechanisms that can cause emotional dysregulation and become the root of communication and behavior patterns that are deleterious to our 'present-day self'. Most of those traumas stem from childhood, but some can develop later. Parts are equally annoyed that they are stuck in the past. Since they can't change that, they do a good job of fooling us into thinking the reactions they have are OK.

When we get triggered we bring these feelings, emotions, and behaviors, because that part of us, that broken boy inside, is afraid we won't survive. Anger is one of the most common and vicious parts that become a coping mechanism.

If I were to use myself as an example, certain parts developed very early in my childhood.

A few days before my third birthday, tragedy struck. My pregnant mother was strangled, raped, and killed. As an eight-month-pregnant woman, she carried my unborn sister. That little boy inside me never got to see his mother again or meet his baby sister.

I may be able to talk about it now, but I sure wasn't able to talk about it until I engaged in my healing journey with my counselor Billy, whom I spoke about earlier in the book.

The pain that was created from that tragedy, also created parts of me that were used as shields from the pain. For so long, vulnerability did not feel as if it was an option, nor was discussing these emotions associated with my pain.

The little boy who never met his sister and who longed for his mother was frozen in that state, confused, and abandoned. Even now, when that broken little boy in me feels triggered as it relates to abandonment or confusion, he can become angry. I need to remain aware of that in my present life, so the anxious and angry energy doesn't hurt my daily life, relationships, and family.

I don't know what your story is, I don't know what pain you've faced in your life. I don't know what the context of your parts is. But I can say that if you have experienced trauma and have not yet engaged on your healing journey, there is likely a part of you, a broken little boy, that is still stuck somewhere.

That little boy will need a lot of love, a lot of reassurance, and a lot of empathy to be re-integrated and soothed. Just like I needed to realize that even though Mom isn't coming home and there is no safety net for him in that regard, he will be safe. Life shifted for me when I was able to help that part of me feel seen, loved, and understood.

My method, even though unconventional, is to speak to the little boy. I still reach out to him in prayer and meditation, to let him know that everything will be okay. I say to him when he is triggered; "I love you, buddy. It's OK. We're OK. We got through this, you're safe now."

After loving this part of me consistently, over a long time, I eventually felt an integration. It's not easy, and it's not fast, but it will happen for you too. Through this integration process, I felt as though a weight was lifted off of my shoulders, allowing me to experience a deeper level of joy, appreciation, and clarity.

The second thing that happened was I was finally ready to bring myself and its parts to my wife. This story is as much mine as it is hers, so I will be expanding later on in the book with her words.

For now, I will say this, though.

When I allowed my wife to talk to that little boy version of me and tell him she loved him, everything changed.

Her request was simple, "Let me love you", but its effects were simply life-changing and magical.

The integration that had started between myself, was now completed and included my life partner.

As I allowed that part of me to be seen, the little boy inside stopped feeling unsafe and scared. He let down its defenses and stopped feeling like he had to fight or run away.

I share this to give you *hope*, that once this occurs, other areas of your life will start to appear different as well.

A clear example of that in my life, where it all clicked together after experiencing that integration, was a conversation I had with my grandmother on her 87th birthday. While that part of me was still present, the little boy in me wasn't triggered anymore. Actually the opposite, I was able to love him and appreciate him even more.

She called me on the phone, and I shared a glimpse of the success I've found in my private counseling practice and how I'm paying it forward, helping others overcome their pain.

She told me, "You've been through so much in your life, and I'm so proud of you."

I fought back the tears while on the call with her, but as soon as we hung up, I couldn't hold them back any longer.

Society often portrays crying, especially for men, as a sign of weakness. But for me, it's a signal that I'm deeply connected to my heart, urging me to explore something significant.

So, I embraced the tears, and here's what surfaced:

For the first time, in a long time, I was truly proud of myself. As she told me she was proud of me, I felt that little boy being told "it's OK you're going to be safe, and everything is going to work out great." Hearing it from my grandmother at that moment really solidified that for me.

As we learn to love and value ourselves, we become open to receiving that love from others- *for all parts of ourselves*. This journey of healing the broken pieces within us, helps us unlock the ability to accept love from the world around us. And that's a powerful transformation.

Actionable Steps

Here are a few questions to reflect on as you begin to work on the inner child we all have inside.

1. **Questions for reflection**
   - Do you see aspects of your inner child in your responses and communication patterns? Note them down.
   - Can you identify coping mechanisms that might have developed during that time?
   - If you could talk to the child version of you, what would you say and how would you say it? Write a letter and share the wisdom of your years.
   - Are you inviting your partner to be part of this journey, allowing them to express love and support to your inner child?
   - Can you embrace a sense of safety and security as your inner child feels seen, loved, and understood, nurturing a more open and connected relationship dynamic?

It's a Team Effort

This chapter will be a bit different. While writing this book, I welcomed, sought, and was inspired by my wife's input and creative thinking. I also wanted to address the idea that 'we counselors have it all figured out.' I promise, we don't, and the truth is, we too deal with similar thoughts, feelings, emotions and relationship struggles.

In the following sections, I've asked my wife to put her thoughts, experiences, and memories into her own words, so there is a clear representation of our process and growth as a couple. Here is what she had to say.

Ryan: Can you share your experience seeing my cry and how it affected you?

Johanna: The first time I saw you cry, I felt uncertain about how to react. I didn't know what to say or if I should say anything. I realized that not only were you the first man that I saw crying, but it also created a feeling of safety. It created a strong bond and feeling in my heart to know that crying is okay in our relationship.

Ryan: That's beautiful! So my crying made you feel safer? Even though society tells us that we need to be strong warrior men who don't cry. Can you expand on that a bit?

Johanna: Absolutely. Your vulnerability stripped away any pretense. You were no longer wearing that mask and that image that I have of you. He's crying. He feels safe with me. We are safe to cry together. It signaled that it's okay to be authentic and emotional, and that I can remove my mask and do the same as well. It's not about showing weakness; it's about being genuine.

Ryan: I recall one instance after my last master's program class when I couldn't hold back my tears. Do you remember that call?

Johanna: I remember it very well. You barely said hi before tears flowed. I was so touched that I found myself crying along with you. It's about forming that deep heart-to-heart connection, feeling what your partner feels. It taught me that I don't need to understand why you're crying or say the perfect words. Just being present and listening is what matters. I think 90% of the times you have cried, I have cried with you and just been present. Not worrying about telling you to stop crying, or what I am supposed to do, just being there. I've also witnessed all different types of tears: joy, appreciation, sadness, and frustration. They all come out in different ways.

Ryan: Can you also share a bit about how my grieving process, related to my mom and sister, impacted you?

Johanna: Sure, it was a learning experience. I realized your wounds from childhood were related to abandonment. Understanding that helped me support you and show that I wouldn't leave you alone in your emotional struggles. The other thing I know is that we all have childhood wounds. If we learn to identify the wounds our partners have, we can walk with them or walk them through a situation when needed. With you, realizing you were afraid of being loved and being abandoned was a huge one. But I also knew I had to ask you to let me love you and show you that I was not going to abandon you.

Ryan: Did my crying about my mom and sister's passing help you understand my fears better, or maybe when my guards are up?

Johanna: Absolutely. It showed me that grief doesn't have a set duration; it's ongoing and varies in intensity. Recognizing this allowed me to better understand your emotional journey. It is going to take, however long it takes. Maybe even forever. Plus, it is going to come up in different ways and levels. Your partner is always going to be grieving at different times in his life. All they need is your presence just to be there and to be with that person.

Ryan: When I cried during grieving moments, did you find it easier to empathize with me? How would you explain it to other women who are reading and trying to do something similar? Was there an "aha" moment to understand, "Hmm, this is why he is doing what he is doing."?

Johanna: Definitely. Connecting my maternal instincts helped me understand how your childhood affected you. It guided me in supporting you and your emotions. I am always connected to my motherly side and being a mother of three. I always think about that and see you in that. My motherly side kicks in, and I realize that not having your mother at the beginning, would have had a tremendous impact on you because I can relate to that when I see my kids and imagine them going through it.

Ryan: How can women support men in expressing their emotions more comfortably? What are the strategies or skills you would recommend?

Johanna: One crucial thing to avoid is weaponizing your partner's feelings by using them against them or making fun of them. Once that happens, it lingers, making it difficult for your partner to open up again. If I had mocked you or belittled your emotions during times when you cried, it would have blocked that vulnerability. You might have felt uncomfortable sharing your emotions, feeling misunderstood or ridiculed. Understanding and acknowledging the emotions without needing to fully comprehend them is key in supporting a partner through tough moments.

Regarding counselors or healthcare professionals, there's a common misconception that they're flawless, knowing all the answers. Kind of like, since you are a counselor, you are perfect and our communication is perfect. However, I've come to realize that being human is at the core of our experiences and emotions. Witnessing you in various emotional states taught me that even therapists make mistakes and have moments of emotional intensity. We're on a journey of learning and communication, where both of us are allowed to make mistakes. Understanding that and dropping the expectation of perfection has been key to our relationship's progress. Embracing imperfections and working together on our relationship has been the driving force for growth.

Ryan: As someone in the healthcare profession discussing emotions, have you seen me make mistakes in expressing my feelings?

Johanna: Absolutely. I've learned to drop expectations of perfection. We're both human and learning to communicate better. Having difficult conversations helps us grow in our relationship.

Ryan: What's your advice on handling disagreements in relationships?

Johanna: Disagreements are normal. It's about what happens afterward. Embrace those conversations, avoid judgment, and work together to ensure both partners feel seen and heard.

Ryan: Absolutely, embracing imperfections in ourselves and our relationships is crucial. It's okay not to have everything figured out.

Finding a Therapist

There is another aspect of the healing process as it relates to it being a "team effort" outside the relationship with your partner. Remember, it's not our job to be a counselor or a therapist to our spouse or partner. Nor is it healthy. This is where finding a trained mental health professional comes in. As I shared earlier in the book, Billy was my counselor and teammate on my healing journey. In this next part of the book, I'm going to share my thoughts, or guidance, on the process of finding a therapist.

A lot of friends, family, and people I have discussions with ask me how to find a therapist. If you don't have one already, you might have a similar question. After all, if you are reading this book you are likely looking for some solutions to the issues you are facing, whether that be trauma, or other non-serving emotions which are plaguing you.

The first thing I will say is that your healing journey is so worth it.

Finding a counselor or therapist is one of the best things you can do for yourself. The first key is to find somebody that you are comfortable with. I always start my initial sessions with individuals by saying the following, "I don't have everything figured, out and I don't promise to, so if you find a counselor that does, please let me know, because I'd like to make them my counselor! But here's what I do know. I know how to be with people. I know how to be with people in their pain, and how my experiences with pain allow me to be a better listener."

Despite what your fears might say, you can find somebody that you feel comfortable with that will sit in your pain with you as well. I promise you they're out there. I think a good counselor or therapist is the person who doesn't walk the journey for you but walks the journey alongside you. A trusted companion that is there with you on your healing journey with no judgment, and is willing to start and stop, go forwards and backward, and even sideways while you find your healing. Counseling and the healing journey are not linear, and no one gets to tell you how long that process should take or exactly how it needs to look for you.

Not every therapist or counselor will match your energy and needs. Expect this to happen. Go on one or two sessions and bring your true self. Most therapists will offer free introductory meetings, or a quick 15-chat on the phone, to see if they're a good fit for you. Notice how your body is feeling during these brief introduction meetings. Are you comfortable? That's a good way to see if you two could be a good fit.

Be present with your wants, needs, values, and expectations. Seek someone who makes you feel seen and heard. You want a balance of someone who validates and listens to you but will also challenge your viewpoints and be able to steer you back to what needs to be done.

My second piece of advice is to lean into the healing process. This can be uncomfortable and strange when it first happens. Think back to the example we discussed about muscles that have never been used.

Every therapist utilizes a different therapeutic toolbox. This is due to their experience, both personal and professional, studies and specialties. Some might offer art therapy, while others specialize in mindfulness or body-based approaches. Don't say no to things before you have tried them. If possible, try a few things and journal or meditate on how the process fits with your needs.

You are never obliged to continue with a therapist if something doesn't click. They are professionals, their feelings won't get hurt. As a matter of fact, most therapists do, or at least should, approach this topic after the first or second session. If you don't feel comfortable, it is okay to find someone else.

My last suggestion is to think about therapy as a playlist. Some days you need a soothing melody to unwind to and others an energizing beat to motivate you. Find the counselor who has a general vibe that resonates the most with you and who can offer that customized flow based on your specific needs.

Connections form the fabric of our lives and weave together moments that influence us for years. So, during your search for a counselor, think about the times you felt profoundly connected to someone. For me, what helps is thinking about Tracy Chapman's song "Fast Car", yes, seriously!

Its chorus embodies a potent message about the power of connection— the feeling of belonging when embraced by someone, a sensation of being valued and recognized. The feeling of being someone. When I think back to the deepest relationships I've had in my life, that feeling of being able to believe in myself and the sense of real connection and love shines through brightly.

As a counselor and a participant in counseling, I've experienced the transformative journey of therapy and witnessed how it can completely alter the course of someone's life. I have also seen what happens when people get that person who believes in them and makes them feel worthy.

Never forget that we, as humans, crave connections, a sense of belonging, and purpose. Seeking a therapist who values this vulnerability and fosters genuine connections is pivotal. They can serve as a guide, helping build that network of authentic connections and supporting you on the journey towards emotional well-being and fulfilling relationships.

BONUS:
Divine Masculine and Divine Feminine

We are at the end of the book, and it is time to deliver on what I promised in the beginning. The reason I left this chapter for this end, is that some might find this topic too spiritual or esoteric, and I get that. I've been vulnerable throughout this book, so I'll be the first to say it. If you'd mentioned the concept of Divine Masculine or Divine Feminine to me before 2019, I would not have been open to it.

I was simply too many steps behind an open mind and heart, to approach the subject with any curiosity. But this may not be the case for you, I hope. So here is what I will tell you.

We can conceptualize the Divine Feminine as an inherent, fundamental female nature and the Divine Masculine as an inherent male energy or way of being. Just as women embody both the Divine Feminine and Divine Masculine, men have access to both too.

Before you start cringing, I encourage you to think about the nurturing instinct fathers feel when their child is sick or hurt. It is almost like a different part inside of you is activated. That's tapping into the Divine Feminine. It's like having both estrogen and testosterone in our bodies, albeit in smaller amounts. (And yes, both men and women have both estrogen and testosterone.)

Men are wired with a natural propensity for having more masculine energy, while women are typically more connected to feminine, nurturing energy. Their energies though, are complementary, like the yin and yang. While it's healthy for men to predominantly live in their Masculine Energy, accessing the Divine Feminine - or as we have defined it throughout most of this book 'connecting into our heart' - makes us unstoppable.

I've witnessed men connecting with their softer, nurturing side and women embracing their power and voice inside therapy. It's awe-inspiring and creates a magnetic force around the individual. Being in touch with both aspects of ourselves is potent. It's about finding balance in relationships, with the man authentically embracing his Masculine power and the woman in her Feminine strength. This balance is not just great for the individual, but it breeds incredible harmony and intimacy for a couple.

For us guys, this means being the strong, protecting, and providing man, who makes the woman in our life feel protected, without being overly suffocated or afraid.

But it's crucial to understand each other's energetic space in communication. Men often reside in their Masculine energy, and women in their Feminine. Without awareness, we miss each other, leading to disconnection. Similar to what we discussed about left and right brain activation, we are dealing with a situation where contrasting parts of our personalities need to come together and work together. Being flexible and knowing when to tap into different energies is transformative in communication and relationships. It is being able to say, "What is it that I need to be able to access right now?" and "Where is it that I need to be, to be able to facilitate this communication?".

The Divine Masculine or masculine energy embodies a physical nature. Men inherently bring security, safety, organization, and direction; they're protectors and provide focus to those around them. This inclination explains why men often excel or naturally gravitate towards roles like firefighters, law enforcement officers, military personnel, or first responders. It's a space where the Divine Masculine thrives, offering its inherent power. Now be careful, assertiveness is confidence in expressing thoughts, not seeking control over others or situations. Strength is about resilience and the ability to endure challenges, not reacting to situations with hostility, anger, or violence. There are many other examples around the key traits we have discussed here, and all of them relate to healthy expression.

Now, let's consider the Divine Feminine. It's more free-flowing, deeply connected to energy and intuition, nurturing, and highly creative—a way of thinking that's outside the box. The magic happens when the Divine Masculine compliments this energy. While the Divine Feminine brings in the creative building blocks, the Divine Masculine structures, and shapes, and keeps things secure.

Since we touched on the toxic aspect of 'toxic masculinity' or an excess of the Divine Masculine energy, I'll offer a few examples of the Divine Feminine. When we talk about nurturing, we are discussing caregiving, compassion, and empathy. The unhealthy version of that is passivity, where a woman would be submissive without asserting her needs and opinions.

Another example is collaboration vs manipulation. The first values relationships and wants to foster connection. The latter uses emotional intelligence and knowledge to take control of relationships.

Imagine the Divine Feminine as the creative force while the Divine Masculine acts as the architect and foundation setter, ensuring safety and direction during the construction process. You want to bring as many of the positive aspects of your power into that equation, instead of the negative ones.

Aspect	Divine Feminine	Divine Masculine
Healthy		
Nurturing	Providing care, compassion, and empathy	Offering protection and a sense of safety
Intuition	Trusting inner wisdom and emotional depth	Logical and strategic thinking
Creativity	Embracing innovation and creative pursuits	Establishing structure and order
Collaboration	Building connections and fostering community	Asserting leadership and decisiveness
Sensitivity	Displaying strength through vulnerability	Demonstrating strength through action
Unhealthy		
Passivity	Being overly submissive or passive	Dominating or overly aggressive behavior

Over-emotional	Allowing emotions to overwhelm and dictate	Suppressing emotions or lack of emotional expression
Manipulation	Using emotional intelligence for control	Using power to dominate or control
Needy	Leads with insecurity and a need for love	Needs to always be right, blame, and shame others
Labels	Sees herself as a victim	Sees himself as Mr. Known it All
Self-sacrifice	Sacrificing oneself excessively for others	Demonstrating excessive self-centeredness
Dependency	Relying too heavily on others for validation	Overly self-reliant or isolating behavior

For a stable structure, both energies need to work together. In relationships, there's a dance—an understanding of when to tap into each energy for effective communication. Men might need to step into their Feminine energy for healthy and vulnerable communication. Whereas women might assert themselves with strength from tapping into their Divine Masculine, while still residing mainly in their feminine space. This energetic or emotional flexibility fosters a deep connection.

In my work with couples, the imbalance between these energies can disrupt relationships. When the Masculine energy dominates or the feminine feels unsafe, walls are built, leading to disconnection. Recognizing when to connect emotionally and communicate vulnerably, even for brief periods, helps maintain safety and prevents these walls from rising.

This is a common occurrence for couples in therapy. For example, let's say a couple is discussing household responsibilities. The man frequently dismisses the woman's opinions, asserting his dominance. He might say things like, "I don't have time for this. I provide for us; that should be enough."

Alternatively, when the woman might bring up a need for connection and more time spent on their own to reconnect their romance, he might blurt, "But we just had sex last week, what more do you need?".

On their own, they might not mean much, but they do add up. When one partner frequently hears, "You're overreacting again. It's not that big of a deal." or "If you'd just listen and stop nagging, we wouldn't be fighting." then the disconnect becomes larger and larger.

Of course, women can and do get things wrong all the time as well. Their unhealthy versions can look like this.

- "I guess I'll just do it myself; as usual, no one helps me."
- "I work so hard, but nobody seems to appreciate it. I'll just keep on doing everything without a good word."
- "If you loved me, you'd do what I ask without questioning it."
- "If you don't do this for me, I'll have to reconsider our relationship."
- "Nothing's wrong; I'm fine. Don't worry about it."

The unhealthy Divine Feminine can be manipulative or needy, instill fear in her partner, or fail to communicate at all. All these responses have various roots that need to be addressed to improve the connection.

Big Boys Do Cry

The language around this may seem esoteric or spiritual to some, but I've witnessed its impact in my counseling sessions. Replacing "Divine Masculine" with "masculine power" and "Divine Feminine" with "female power" might resonate more with some readers. I once thought this sounded hokey too, but I've seen its significance in relationships firsthand.

Take what resonates with you, and feel free to leave behind what doesn't.

I Got You, Man

You made it to the end.

Before I say anything else, let me say, thank you for coming this far with me. I truly appreciate your time and openness to read these words.

I honor the heck out of you for being open to what was shared on these pages.

The next step that I invite you to explore is to take the parts of this book that resonate with you and begin to implement them into your life. You can start with browsing through your favorite chapters, and then noting some actionable steps that speak to you.

At the same time, if there are parts of this book that don't resonate, feel free to completely disregard them. There is no one-size-fits-all manual. We are different human beings, with our unique set of lived experiences that impact the way we view the world.

You've got your experiences, and I've got mine, shaping how we see things. If parts of my story resonate with you, awesome. If not, that's cool too. No pressure.

But I want you to know something—I've got your back.

I see you.

I hear you.

I'm here, just holding space.

And hey, change? Totally possible.

Big Boys Do Cry

Maybe I'm a bit biased, but I think there's some pretty solid stuff here that might help spark that change in you and your relationships.

This book, I hope, nudged you to open up, to feel that heart connection, and to bring more vulnerability to your connections. Healing? Yeah, it's not a straight line. It's like this journey full of starts, stops, moments when we sprint, and moments where we stumble. That's the ride.

Give yourself grace and compassion as you move through the process, understanding that there may be periods when you feel that you're going forward and then other times where you are going backward. You're not!

And those moments when you realize you've slipped back into old patterns? That's part of the process too. It's when we lose sight of that, that we stall.

You know, from a lot of what I've shared, I'm right there with ya in the mix too. It's ongoing work. Sometimes I nail it, other times I miss big. I'm still learning. Imperfect, just like you. That's the truth I hope you have felt through my honesty here.

I hope these words help you to love yourself and the people closest to you at an even deeper level.

Love ya my brothers,

Ryan

Made in the USA
Columbia, SC
14 March 2024

33047308R00078